Appreciative Coaching

Sara L. Orem
Jacqueline Binkert
Ann L. Clancy

JB JOSSEY-BASS

Appreciative Coaching

A Positive Process for Change

John Wiley & Sons, Inc.

Published by Jossey-Bass
A Wiley Imprint
989 Market Street, San Francisco, CA 94103-1741   www.josseybass.com

Jossey-Bass books and products are available through most bookstores. To contact Jossey- Bass directly call our Customer Care Department within the U.S. at 800-956-7739, outside the U.S. at 317-572-3986, or fax 317-572-4002.

Jossey-Bass also publishes its books in a variety of electronic formats. Some content that appears in print may not be available in electronic books.

Library of Congress Cataloging-in-Publication Data

Orem, Sara L., date.
    Appreciative coaching : a positive process for change / Sara L. Orem,
Jacqueline Binkert, Ann L. Clancy.
       p. cm. — (The Jossey-Bass business & management series)
    Includes bibliographical references and index.
    ISBN-13: 978-0-7879-8453-3
       1. Executive coaching. 2. Organizational change. I. Binkert, Jacqueline.
II. Clancy, Ann L. III. Title.
    HD30.4.O74 2007
    658.3'124—dc22   2006035778

Printed in the United States of America
FIRST EDITION
HB Printing   10 9 8 7 6 5 4 3

Contents

Foreword

In the early 1980s at Case Western Reserve University, I was part of a small group of scholars, including David Cooperrider, Suresh Srivastva, and Ron Fry, who were experimenting with an appreciative approach to organizational life. Led by David Cooperrider, we were frustrated with the widespread acceptance and use of problem solving in action research and organization development. The beginnings of our work focused on what was good in organizations and on what and who worked well and effectively together. As this philosophy became more widely known, many people were drawn to it because of its positive, even uplifting focus. Other researchers, organization development consultants, government workers, and project managers began to apply Appreciative Inquiry in their work. The three authors of this book came to know Appreciative Inquiry in this way, through their own work in organizations.

They found, as we did, that focusing on what is life giving now so that something even greater can be made from it in the future has transformed the way people think about organizational change. What makes this book unique is the innovative way the authors have applied the principles and stages of Appreciative Inquiry to the realm of coaching, transforming the way people think about individual change and the coaching relationships which enable that change. They have built an Appreciative Coaching model based on sound coaching research and have grounded their approach in a solid theoretical foundation that includes not only Appreciative Inquiry but also Positive Psychology, Positive Organizational Scholarship, and other positive psychological theories of change and time.

This is an exciting new application of Appreciative Inquiry and one that I think will make an impact in the field of organization development and coaching. The interest in Appreciative Inquiry and other affirmative modes of inquiry has grown beyond Case Western Reserve University, where this research began. Other similar centers of learning and practice have sprung up, such as the Taos Institute and Positive Organizational Scholarship at the University of Michigan Business School. The appreciative approach to coaching expands on the meaning and significance of the five core principles underlying Appreciative Inquiry (Constructionist Principle, Positive Principle, Simultaneity Principle, Poetic Principle, and Anticipatory Principle) and creates a new foundation for enabling positive, transformative change in individuals.

The authors explore each of the five principles and provide suggestions and client stories to ensure that readers understand not only the theoretical underpinnings of positive individual change but also how to apply the principles in a concrete manner. I was delighted to see that the Appreciative Coaching principles, like those in Appreciative Inquiry, reflect a worldview, not of a fixed and determined machinelike universe, but of one that is open, dynamic, interconnected, and filled with possibilities.

What Appreciative Inquiry has offered to organizations and individuals over the past twenty years is an alternative to focusing on problems and to problem solving. An overdependence on a problem perspective can result in cases of solving the wrong problem or of solving one problem only to find that a more serious problem has arisen out of the solution to the original one. For example, in executive coaching, where there is typically a more positive focus on strengths, a continued emphasis on individual weaknesses in the development of corporate talent is still pervasive. As we have found after working with thousands of different organizations, the positive energy created in an appreciative process is very different from the energy created in solving a problem, no matter how important the solution of that problem may be. An appreciative process allows for the unfolding of innovation and creativity based on a positive foundation. It is energizing for people to think about, dream about, and talk about the things they do well and enjoy! Building on these things is very often easier than enabling incremental improvement in something they or someone else has identified as a weakness.

Consultants, coaches, and managers seek tools to address the increased complexity of personal and organizational life. Having witnessed and participated in the palpable energy created by an Appreciative Inquiry initiative in groups, the authors of this book have crafted a remarkable model for coaching that uses the best of this perspective with individual clients to create and sustain the energy needed to act into a more positively envisioned future.

Drawing from their experience with Appreciative Inquiry, the authors have adapted the four key stages of Appreciative Inquiry into their Appreciative Coaching approach: Discovery, Dream, Design, and Destiny. They then expand on the core stages to present an authoritative yet insightful process for engaging in Appreciative Coaching. They skillfully weave together concepts, client stories, suggestions, and tools for incorporating an appreciative approach into an existing or new coaching practice.

The Discovery stage is about truly appreciating what gives life to clients and helping them acknowledge an appreciative view of themselves. The coach specifically helps clients focus on the life-giving forces and root causes of their current and past successes using four core appreciative questions. In the Dream stage, the coach guides clients to explore their longings and concrete desires for an even more successful future. This stage enables clients to experience a unique sense of coherence to their lives because their dream is grounded in and extends from their own past and present. During the Design stage, the coach helps clients direct their attention and take action so that they become the designers of the future they most desire. Finally, in the Destiny stage, clients learn to recognize and celebrate their dream and to live their lives fully and well.

Karen Armstrong, one of our most cogent thinkers about the divisions caused by world religions, writes in *The Spiral Staircase*, "The one and only test of a valid religious idea, spiritual experience, or devotional practice is that it must lead directly to practical compassion." What Appreciative Coaching does is to put this practical compassion at the forefront of each stage of the coaching relationship, making sure that together, coach and client discover each accomplishment and prideful recollection, dream each future with care and attention, design experiments that are fun, and deliver clients to their destiny having both learned about themselves and their world and created lasting change!

Experienced coaches will want to add appreciative processes to their own already expert practices. Newer coaches may want to adopt Appreciative Coaching as their core philosophy. All coaches, managers who coach, and people interested in self-coaching will learn how to celebrate their own wisdom and to leverage that wisdom to achieve greater and more satisfactory results in their lives and in the lives of their clients and employees. The authors provocatively suggest that coaching processes based on Appreciative Inquiry engage people more completely because the focus is on the positive present and possible future, rather than on the problems of the past and present. Who wouldn't want to participate in such a series of coaching conversations?

Reference

Armstrong, K. (2004). *The spiral staircase: My climb out of darkness*. New York: Anchor, p. 293.

Frank J. Barrett, Ph.D.
Professor of Management
Graduate School of Business and Public Policy
Naval Postgraduate School
Monterey, California 93943
fbarrett@nps.edu

Acknowledgments

First, we acknowledge David Cooperrider, Frank Barrett, Suresh Srivastva, Jackie Stavros, and the many, many others who showed us the power of Appreciative Inquiry (AI). We thank the Fielding Graduate University and the International Coach Federation for giving us a "playing field" and an audience of colleagues, supporters, and fellow coaches. The International Coach Federation also provided us a scholarly conference in which to present and test our theory.

Positive Links at the University of Michigan, the fluid group that studies and practices together using the principles of Positive Organizational Scholarship, provided more opportunities to learn and network with scholars working with other positive methods, and a community of practice in which we could question, try out, and dream our own dream.

Sara thanks Frank Barrett, a cocreator of AI and an early guide, and Jackie Stavros, for their instruction, encouragement, and support. She is also in debt to two book writing groups, and especially to Rich Snowden for comments early and late, and Leslie Quinn. Murray, her husband, suffered her absence or anxiety with good humor and good advice.

Jackie thanks her family, friends, and colleagues for supporting and encouraging her, forgiving her absences, and holding a place for her return. She thanks her husband, Peter, not only for the gifts of love and support but especially for his gift of time and talent on behalf of this project when he might have been listening to opera or enjoying the Florida sun.

Ann thanks her coach Bobette Reeder for her unflagging support over the years and for being a wonderful model of positive coaching. She also thanks her husband, Gene, and daughter, Coco, for their love and understanding, and friends Sarie and Linda for their support.

We could not have done this work without the early enthusiasm of Neal Maillet, our editor at Jossey-Bass, and Bernadette Walter, also of Jossey-Bass, who saw the idea as a viable possibility and referred us to Neal.

Our clients, both those who participated in our formal research and those who have joined our practice since, deserve our most heartfelt thanks. They have helped us see more clearly what we intend and what we are able to do as Appreciative Coaches. Our coders confirmed that we were using Appreciative Inquiry consistently and visibly in our second phase of research. We thank Linda Blong, Steve Wallis, and George Johnstone for their generous donation of time, thoughtfulness, and accurate attention to a detailed job.

Peter Binkert, theoretical linguist and editor extraordinaire, not only helped us identify a consistent voice and style but also asked us questions about our stories, our method, and our collaboration that caused us to think more deeply. Although all of the work is our responsibility, that it is as clear as it is should be credited to Peter.

Introduction

Certainty is often an illusion, and repose is not the destiny of man.

> Aristotle (384–322 B.C.), Greek philosopher,
> teacher of Alexander the Great

Who of us can forget that feeling of wonder and excitement when as children we first looked into a kaleidoscope? Suddenly we were privy to an incredible world of color and patterns that kept changing as we turned it. Nothing on the outside could prepare us for the images we saw on the inside. What a mystery it seemed to glimpse a whole other world, visible only through a tiny hole!

Invented in 1816 by a child prodigy, Sir David Brewster of Scotland, kaleidoscopes are enjoying a resurgence of popularity in the twenty-first century. For some collectors and aficionados, the kaleidoscope is a metaphor for wholeness and integration. The instrument is tube shaped and contains mirrors set at different angles to reflect the image of loose pieces of glass and other colorful objects, creating symmetrical patterns. Looking through the eyepiece, the viewer can turn the tube to see different patterns. A kaleidoscope can generate infinite numbers of images, yet focuses the mind in such a way that one sees into a new perceptual frontier, an experience that demonstrates the unity and interrelatedness of form into an organic whole—but just for an instant! One nudge of the tube, and that image is erased and a new one produced. Brewster, who was greatly delighted with his new device, named it using the Greek words *kalos* ("beautiful"), *eidos* ("form"), and *scopos* ("watcher"): the beautiful form-watcher.

In this book, we will describe an approach to coaching that has its roots in Appreciative Inquiry. The essence of this approach—called Appreciative Coaching—is captured by the metaphor of Brewster's kaleidoscope image because it is an exciting way to help clients discover the positive possibilities inherent within them. We have seen how with just subtle shifts in self-perception, clients become watchers of their own (beautiful) ability to be more self-integrated and bring form to their deeply held dreams. Of course, one hopes that such shifts in self-perception are built into all good coaching approaches. What makes the appreciative approach unique for us is that its core principles are designed to show individuals how to tap into (or rediscover) their childlike sense of wonder and excitement about their present life and future possibilities.

Our Desire with This Book

We were drawn to create this appreciative approach to coaching by the desire to help our clients create more meaningful lives in a way that would be inspirational and exciting, yet gentle. How could we help nurture the miraculous process of change and discovery in our clients in a way that would be self-affirming and nonjudgmental for them? How could we help clients awaken to their deepest dreams and desires while at the same time help them see their own inner strengths and abilities to realize those desires?

We were inspired to develop our Appreciative Coaching approach because each of us, on our separate paths, experienced the marvel of a shift in perception. It turned out to be a profound shift for each of us, especially given our backgrounds. All three of us have doctorates and extensive experience in the field of organization development. We were originally trained to view the organizations we worked with as problems to be solved. Our job was to prompt executives, managers, and teams to identify their problems, and then to facilitate their finding solutions. By focusing on problems, our clients sometimes had difficulty thinking beyond them. Things improved for us when we began incorporating the concept of vision into our work, but it still felt as if we were missing a positive, life-enhancing way to work with our clients. Although we were often successful in bringing about change, we did not always see evidence of excitement and passion on the part of our clients.

That changed, however, when each of us discovered and began incorporating into our own work the Appreciative Inquiry approach to change, which is based on a very different premise, one that views organizations as miracles to be embraced and as mysteries to be explored. This appreciative approach significantly changed how we began to interact with our clients. It seemed as though we suddenly saw our clients in new and unique ways. Organizations weren't problems anymore—they were whole entities that were inherently successful. Although they did some things "wrong," they did a whole lot more that was right. We now had the tools to inspire people to explore what they found most meaningful in their work and to share that with others in the workplace.

Sara was the first to realize that this wonderful new approach to change might be equally profound applied to one-on-one coaching relationships. Together, we set out to explore this premise in a coaching research project[1] that culminated in the development of this process we call Appreciative Coaching.

Our Common Roots in Coaching

Coaching as it is being practiced today is a new field. Its rapid growth is an indication that it is tapping into a fundamental need to make people's lives and work more meaningful, balanced, and holistic. The roots of the professional practice burrow deep into the fields of education, psychology, athletics, organization development, and communication studies. Postmodern philosophies, such as social constructionism, influence how we think about the nature of reality[2] and our ability to assist clients in creating their preferred future. People come to the study and practice of coaching from one or more of its root fields. They have been scholars, managers, actors, psychotherapists, and many other things, and they bring all the richness of their history and experience to our profession. Given their roots, coaches usually find a groove or a core methodology they trust and depend on to practice coaching.

Pioneers have forged a way for us. In athletics, Tim Gallwey demonstrated that coaching as a method was distinct from the discipline of teaching.[3] Thomas Leonard, founder of modern coaching, forged new ground in bringing coaching into both the personal and business arenas. Since Leonard established the first CoachU school, many others have sprung up to enrich the field and encourage new practitioners to join the ranks of practice in a professional, competent manner. Universities are now setting up academic degree programs in coaching.

Coaches have begun to move away from relying on their intuition and the discovery of techniques and are calling for evidence-based research that demonstrates what truly works for their clients. Professional coaching associations sponsor research symposiums both in the United States and Europe; universities support research through their students' doctoral dissertations; coaches worldwide are raising their level of expertise by supporting high standards in the profession. The influence and prestige of the field as an academic discipline has consequently grown.

Ann has been an adult educator, business writer, professional facilitator, and organization development consultant; her roots are in education, linguistics, and human and organizational systems. She has studied and incorporated action-oriented and developmental coaching in her work with professionals and executives, drawing frequently on her organization development background prior to coming to Appreciative Coaching.

Jackie has been an adult educator and organization development consultant. Her roots are in linguistics, adult learning, organizational learning, and human and organizational systems. Her work has also combined organization development with executive coaching.

Sara has been a salesperson, nonprofit manager, and director of organization development. Her roots are in communication studies, theology, and human and organizational systems. She has taught performance coaching (action-oriented) within a master's management program and has also studied developmental methods.

Our diverse backgrounds have enabled us to bring a varied perspective to our work with clients. Our research has culminated in an appreciative approach to coaching that draws its inspiration from a vast literature in a variety of fields and from the many workshops we have attended in other strength-based and ontological coaching methods.

Our Paths to an Appreciative Approach

Although each of us came to Appreciative Inquiry (hereafter, AI) along different paths, we found that we all embraced it for the same reasons: its underlying principles and philosophy around positive change.

Sara's Story

Sara first became interested in and experienced with this methodology in her work with groups in corporations. For many years her career included facing mostly angry groups of people in large forums. As the change agent in several corporations, she was the messenger bearing bad news: "We have to change. We have to change now." The owners wanted it, or the economy demanded it, or the market for the product was shrinking. People in these auditoriums and conference rooms sat stone-faced, arms folded protectively across their chests, eyebrows knit, immovable. They had heard bad news and been told they had to change before.

Then Sara discovered a new way to begin this process of learning and change, one based on AI. When she started to use the method with large groups, she found a completely different response to her message. People sat up in their chairs. They smiled at each other and dug into the questions about past history, current reality, and future possibilities. They reported feeling much more personal power around embarking on the change process, and they were excited to begin to answer the engaging questions and to define the necessary changes. In fact, they were excited about creating the changes.

Although this enthusiastic response to the need for change certainly made Sara's job easier, it also made her a little wary. How could asking about people's past successes and future longings elicit such a different and positive energy? If the energy she was part of was so powerful in large groups of people, could it be as effective with just one other person? She studied AI further and began to adapt its core questions into her coaching practice as a way to engage people in their dreams and designs for different futures. She also began to think about sharing her initial research and experience with other coaches in hopes of developing and testing Appreciative Coaching as a new coaching method. In the course of this networking, she invited Jackie and Ann to join her in the development of the approach.

Jackie's Story

Jackie views her path to Appreciative Coaching as intertwined with the journey of her life. She felt a strong inner motivation to take advantage of certain events and possibilities as they presented themselves to lead her to a way of working and being that she loves. The time of the greatest change in her work began in the late 1980s when she made a career shift from adult education to organization development. She was fortunate at that time to have gifted teachers and mentors who taught her the value of understanding the present and creating a preferred future before deciding on action steps toward that future. Working with them, she designed programs that brought forth clients' excitement about what was possible.

In 1990, she began working at Ford Motor Company as an internal consultant. There she was given the opportunity to collaborate with such leading thinkers as Peter Senge, author of The Fifth Discipline. Working with him and his colleagues in bringing organizational learning to Ford, Jackie expanded her learning and her methods for integrating the benefits and value of self-understanding and mastery into her consulting work with clients. As she progressed in her career, she was aware of AI but skeptical of its exclusive focus on the positive, especially in the initial phases of working with clients. Although she agreed with the underlying principle that "we get more of what we focus on" and even taught this principle to clients when talking about vision, she had difficulty reconciling it with her value of being honest with oneself about the past and present. These two principles were in conflict for her.

Interestingly, opportunities for understanding this dichotomy kept presenting themselves to her in the form of individuals who were having great success using AI. As she heard more about its positive results, she gradually began to recognize how aligned she already was with its philosophy and practices. So when Sara asked her to join in researching the application of AI principles to coaching, it seemed a perfect opportunity. It allowed Jackie to explore in depth how an appreciative approach worked for her and to learn in a way that best suited her style. She already believed in the power of focusing on the positive and on creating an image of the future. This offer gave her a way—through researching, experimenting, reflecting, and writing— to bring her education and experience together and finally to reconcile the conflicts inherent in her previous approaches. The experience moved her beyond an intellectual grasp of principles to an inner understanding of how empowering it can be to affirm and enhance one's own strengths.

Ann's Story

Ann first began using AI in her strategic planning efforts with organizations. Like Sara, she worked with managers who were by and large skeptical that any real change would occur as a result of their efforts. They had had plenty of past experiences in which the planning either petered out for lack of energy and momentum or ended with reports left on shelves. They had found that too often they got mired in the organization's problems and who or what caused them. Although Ann certainly had success in helping groups identify their problem areas, create a shared vision, and map *out an action plan to move forward, she observed her clients' lack of passion and enthusiasm for the future. It seemed a continual challenge to engage groups as a whole and individuals in particular in ways that generated positive feelings about where they were headed.*

Ann, like Jackie, was also aware of the AI approach but thought it almost too good to be true. Although attracted to its basic positive premises, she was skeptical of its real impact on organizations. How could you avoid talking about the problems organizations faced? What would managers say if she presented them with a planning process that didn't focus primarily on their problems? It seemed too risky. In her personal and professional life, however, Ann was an avid follower of using positive principles and imaging for the future. She was flourishing with her coaching clients and in her own coaching relationship; her coach helped her reframe situations and self-perceptions in more positive ways.

When asked by Jackie and Sara if she would like to join them in researching an appreciative approach to coaching, Ann felt as though fate had intervened. Here was a chance to integrate her professional and personal approaches to change. She began tentatively experimenting with an AI approach to strategic planning that bypassed an emphasis on problem solving and started immediately with what was already working well in the organization. Like Sara, Ann experienced dramatic changes. She could feel the energy rise in the room when people began sharing what they most cared about in the organization and what most inspired them. They told passionate stories about their work and their companies. They smiled and laughed and actually enjoyed talking about the future. Everything just got brighter. Evaluations from the planning sessions strongly supported the use of this method to complete work and connect to each other in a new and powerfully energizing way. Today, Ann incorporates AI principles and stages into all her strategic planning and facilitation projects.

Coming Together

Obviously, the successes we experienced with applying appreciative principles in the realm of organizations and groups emboldened us during our research with individual coaching clients. One of the basic tenets of AI—discover and build on your past and present successes—informed our own research. What seemed remarkable was our similar experiences and results using an appreciative approach. Clearly this approach matched our personal values around change—that by moving forward with a positive intent and believing in the principles, we were responsible for the active construction of our own reality.

Our biases will be evident throughout this book. In a way, the book represents a worldview that three different people found they shared. If you are reading this book because you also share this worldview, we welcome you. If you are reading this book with a healthy dose of skepticism, we applaud you for your curiosity. As you can see from our stories, we were also tentative in our acceptance of this approach.

How to Use This Book

We are excited to share with you the foundation and basis for our approach as well as the many stories from our clients that we've had the privilege to witness. We also talk about our own reflections, thoughts, and experiences in the development of this approach and present concrete steps and actions you can take to incorporate an Appreciative Coaching approach into your existing practice or in building a new practice. As a form of confidentiality for our clients, we have not identified the names of the coaches in the client stories; however, all the client stories involve one of us as the coach. We have also changed the names of some clients.

A wonderful gift of being involved in this effort is the sense of freedom we now feel—freedom from the constraints of viewing our coaching clients in limited or problem-oriented ways. It is very life enhancing for us as coaches to fundamentally believe that we can facilitate the miracle and mystery of life in our own clients.

Each chapter of the book is designed to build the case and to tell the story of our experiences and the positive results of testing and reweaving the AI principles and stages into an Appreciative

Coaching model. For this reason, you are likely to gain the greatest benefit by reading the chapters in order. If you come to this book with substantial experience and knowledge of AI, however, feel free to jump around and read those chapters that call out to you. Our intent in the book is to give future practitioners of Appreciative Coaching all the theory and practical hands-on knowledge and tools they will need to move forward.

In Chapter One, we tell the story of Alan, who made a remarkable journey from frustration and embarrassment over his failing business to a "hugely successful year." Reading this story, you will see examples of many of the elements of the Appreciative Coaching approach described in this overview of our coaching process.

In Chapter Two, we trace the historical roots of the AI change process and other positive methods on which our coaching model is based. As is true of every successful change process, there are fundamental principles involved that guide its theory and practice. We illustrate those principles in Chapters Three and Four in telling our clients' stories of personal and professional transformation and in describing ways to recognize the principles in practice.

Chapter Five offers a concrete outline and the steps for starting an Appreciative Coaching relationship with your clients. Chapters Six through Nine present the four stages of Appreciative Coaching: Discovery, Dream, Design, and Destiny.

In Chapter Ten, we outline the four key steps we followed as we incorporated Appreciative Coaching into our own coaching practices. We suggest ways of incorporating the stages and principles into an existing or new client coaching practice, describing how they can enrich other coaching methods. In the appendixes, we present a summary of our research project, our Client Information Form, and a sample Coaching Prep Form.

We hope you are looking forward to discovering a new way of looking at coaching relationships or enhancing your existing approach.

The Authors

Sara L. Orem, Ph.D., principal of Lotus Coaching, enables the realization of concrete goals as well as long-held dreams for a client base consisting of managers, artists, and graduate business students. She has directed learning and development within large financial services organizations, coached senior executive teams, designed leadership development experiences, and taught Appreciative Coaching within graduate business programs. Her particular research interest is in turning conflict into learning and collaboration.

Jacqueline Binkert, Ph.D., president of Organizational Enterprises, has extensive experience supporting leaders and other professionals to create positive change in both the organizations they serve and their personal lives. Working as an executive coach and organizational development consultant, she has helped her clients deal with such topics as strategic planning, leadership excellence, personal development, and culture change. Her particular interest is in the relationship between the beliefs people have and the results they want.

Ann L. Clancy, Ph.D., president of Clancy Consultants, is an executive coach, organizational development consultant, professional facilitator, and qualitative researcher. She coaches executives, business owners, and professionals from an appreciative approach by leading them to discover, dream, and design their personal and professional lives around their true values and purpose. She specializes in offering an appreciative approach to strategic planning with clients ranging from corporations and governmental agencies to community groups.

Appreciative Coaching

1

An Overview of
Appreciative Coaching

Look with favour upon a bold beginning.
Virgil (70–19 B.C.), Roman epic poet

T he best place to start, most often, is at the beginning. Although there were many beginnings to developing our Appreciative Coaching process together and many beginnings to the work we will describe here, Alan's story seemed just right to introduce you to what this book is all about.

Alan's Story

It started for me when I realized that despite all of my best efforts, I was not making any progress in obtaining enough billable client work to sustain my business. My frustrations and concerns grew to the point that I was beyond worrying about the potential embarrassment of admitting my struggles to friends and colleagues. And then one day it came to me . . . I needed to get some coaching—an objective, outside look into what I was doing, how I was doing it, and how I was being a barrier to my own success. The face of a good friend and colleague popped into my thoughts. I can't explain exactly why she came to mind, other than that the many conversations we've had over the last seven years have led me to respect her thinking, her compassion, and her integrity very much.

Alan's coach also remembers the beginning:

One day in the fall, Alan called to ask if I would meet with him to discuss something of a personal nature. We decided to meet at a local coffee shop, where he told me that he was feeling demoralized because he was unable to make an adequate living doing the work he loved. His situation had become so critical that he would soon be faced with making decisions he did not want to make. He said he worked very hard and gave away a great deal to local community groups and businesses in an effort to make his work known, but the financial benefit was not coming back to him as he had hoped. The situation was serious, if not quite desperate. He was looking to me to see if I could give him some information that might yield insight and ideas for action on his part to change his situation. He did not want to move away from the work he loved and did so well. His clients valued him, his work, and the results they were able to produce because of his interactions with them.

Alan is an organization development consultant in the Detroit area— an area that has been severely depressed economically since the 9/11 attacks. It is an automotive city where the Big Three—General Motors, Ford Motor Company, and DaimlerChrysler—have their corporate headquarters. The economy is dependent on these giants, as many businesses support them through the supply of parts, direct support, and indirect services. When the Big Three do not do well, everyone in Detroit suffers, especially the small service providers like Alan.

Alan and I agreed to an Appreciative Coaching relationship and to meet weekly for an hour. We agreed that the topic for coaching was "making money doing the work he loves."

Discovery

Alan remembers getting started with his coach:

Within a few hours of our agreeing to a process and a start date, she e-mailed me a couple of forms. One was her Client Information Form and the other was a Coaching Prep Form, both of which she asked me to complete before our first session. These forms were an indicator to me that the approach she was using, and the opportunities I would see as a result, were both different from any other I had experienced and very special. These were some of the questions:

- Describe your three greatest accomplishments to date.

- What made these accomplishments stand out for you?

- What have you incorporated into your current actions from your past accomplishments?

- How could you use what you've learned from these accomplishments to assist you in making future changes?

- Who are, or have been, your major role models?

- What attributes of these role models do you admire and most appreciate?

- What are the five most positive things in your life?

- Who are the key supportive people in your life, and what do they provide for you?

- List five adjectives that describe you at your best.

- What energizes you?

- What would you like to contribute to the world?

- What are you most wanting to achieve in the next three years?

These are not the usual sort of questions I see. There was no asking about problems or concerns or issues or anything that was negative. Instead the questions were framed in a positive manner, and as I thought about them, I felt a growing sense of energy and optimism inside myself. I felt good about myself as I answered these questions . . . and even better about the possibility of good things happening for me as a result of the upcoming coaching. This positive energy carried over into our first actual coaching session. I looked forward to the beginning session with great hope *and optimism. I was predisposed to believe that I would find great insights about myself as a result of the questions my coach had already asked and those she would be asking throughout the coaching process. The more I thought about things, the better I felt, and the higher my hopes and expectations soared. The last comment I wrote on my prep form before the initial session was ". . . sort of like I've gotten an injection of positive vibes or something like that."*

The first coaching session with Alan was in person. His coach describes it here:

We went through the four appreciative questions we ask in the first session. Throughout our first meeting, Alan maintained a positive demeanor. Occasionally, the sadness and concern about his business came through, but in general, the questions elicited responses that showed he held great joy in his work. His answers were descriptive and provided rich detail. I believed in his passion for his work and that he made meaningful connections with his clients, serving them well. Even through the positive responses, however, I observed that Alan gave a lot to friends, colleagues, and clients and made very few requests of them. So I asked Alan to consider the flow of giving in each of the stories he told; that is, I asked him to think about the direction of giving and receiving. I was very careful to ask this question in a neutral way. His own startled observation was that the flow was mostly unidirectional, from him to others. I thought about asking him to identify situations where he had made requests that had worked out well, but decided to wait because we needed to take the process at Alan's tempo. He needed time to consider what was clearly a new learning for him. He left our meeting energized by the work we had done and eager to move forward with the coaching process. After this session, I reflected on how important it was to be in a learning mode with our clients, to allow the client to reveal the possibilities for us.

As Alan reports here, the meeting exceeded his already high expectations:

My coach walked me through the Client Information Form by asking probing, positive questions. Partway through this first session, she mentioned that she was seeing something of a trend in my way of being with clients and potential clients, and she asked me a couple of great questions that helped me see the same thing. The insights for me from this first conversation included the following:

- I tend to do a lot of giving to others but not much asking for myself. And, without asking, there isn't much for the universe to work with.

- I was habitually taking on more than 100 percent responsibility for professional relationships.[1]

- I was much more successful in past situations when I only took on 100 percent and made direct requests of others to do the same.

- I should probably be clearer about what I need regarding my requests of others (and the universe).

This was a very powerful and liberating set of learnings for me, and they immediately began having a positive impact on my conscious thinking and behavior. These insights both pushed and pulled me onto a more energized and successful path.

Over the next few sessions, Alan and his coach continued to focus on the issue of taking responsibility and making requests. As they did so, Alan gained even more insights into his own potential. He describes his experience:

The insights gained from our third and fourth sessions were just as amazing and just as valuable for me: whenever I am bold and centered and make requests that benefit both parties, I am more successful. What can I learn from my reflections regarding requests, trends, balance points, feelings, and so on? How can I use this learning to become centered and even more powerful in my behaviors?

My coach continued to ask me very positive, very probing, very challenging questions around all these issues, all the while helping me feel more positive about taking new actions that could achieve more successful outcomes for each issue. Every question, and every agreed-on action, was *geared toward trying something that fit with my strengths, values, and vision and that would lead to positive outcomes.*

Alan shared his insights with his coach. She reports:

By our third session, Alan had a clear and strong understanding of what balance of responsibility felt like and why it was important to him. He shared that realizing how making requests was beneficial both to him and the other party was a turning point for him. He felt great; making clear requests was something that he knew he could do because he had already demonstrated he could. It was not unfamiliar territory.

Dream

As his coach continued to work with Alan, they shifted their focus from immediate awareness of how Alan was changing *in* his business to how he wanted to *change* his business. The coach started moving Alan toward a new dream or vision for his business:

Once the discoveries were well under way, Alan and I shifted to his dream for his business. He started documenting his business life: mission, vision, value, colleagues, clients, revenue, reputation. The list was quite complete and the descriptions very rich.

Alan realized there was a major disconnect between his vision and his behavior in his business partnership. He describes his situation this way:

One example of how this appreciative approach played out for me is the relationship with my business partner. One of the insights I gained from working with my coach is that my vision won't be achieved if I continue to behave in the way I've been behaving with respect to the partnership issue and process. I am not addressing the situation for some reason(s). She began by asking me what I needed and wanted in a business partner. She asked me to create a list. She also coached me through developing a request for my business partner to create his own list around the same question. My business partner and I then shared our respective lists with each other. Our lists were very different, and this prompted us to have a long conversation about those differences, or mismatches. It was one of the best conversations I've had with my business partner in several years . . . very healthy, very personal, very revealing . . . and a relief for both of us to realize that we had been feeling many of the same less-than-happy things related to the professional relationship.

My coach then asked me to review my vision for the business, taking into account the new realizations about the mismatches with my business partner. The resulting vision was much more personal and much more vibrant and full of possibilities than it had been only a few weeks before. She applied the same basic process as she had with the partner needs list . . . she asked me to develop a request for my business partner to create his vision for the business. Again, we shared our respective visions with each other, and discovered even more mismatches. Clearly we were both learning a great deal of extremely critical information about ourselves, our hopes and dreams, and our potential for continuing in a collective business.

In the end, my business partner and I collectively, through reasonable conversation, came to the conclusion that we did not want the same things from and for the business, and that we should not continue on as partners in the business. We parted as professional partners, but remained good friends. I really believe that the partnership would have ended eventually, but without the good feelings and intact friendship. I know that my business partner and I would have ended up in some sort of major conflict had my coach not helped me take only 100 percent responsibility and make reasonable requests of my business partner to do the same. Her questions helped me frame the situation in a very different and very positive light . . . something I had not been able to do for over three years previously.

Alan's coach was proud of the way he moved forward with a new dream for himself:

In painting his future picture, Alan came to realize that the relationship with his business partner was not of the type he dreamed about, but he felt unsure about how to bring this up with him. Following the principles and practices of Appreciative Coaching, Alan decided that it would be ideal for him to engage his partner in his own dream for the business. He felt very capable and eager to lead this discussion. Perhaps not surprisingly, both partners discovered that they were not suited to one another. Happily this process of conversation allowed them to disengage amicably and productively.

Design

Over several months, Alan and his coach crafted a strategy using his strengths and expertise to build his business, being mindful of the balance between his giving to and receiving from his clients. His coach reports:

The coaching meetings were held over the telephone. Each time, Alan provided me with a summary of our coaching conversation, his learnings, and a list of assignments for the coming week. Prior to each session, Alan sent me his Coaching Prep Form and any assignments that were in written form. Alan took coaching very seriously and did everything he could to make the most of it. Together we created an economic exchange process as an application of his new learnings to marketing and sales. It was a process that felt comfortable to him and one that he was eager to try out. In parallel with creating this process, Alan and I also spoke about practical marketing efforts that he could make in the present. We enhanced the implementation of what he already did well with new understanding and experimenting.

During this time, Alan told me several stories of pivotal moments when he came to recognize that the work with his clients was not shared in an appropriate manner. Whenever he raised this concern with a client, they were able to develop a better way to move forward. Relationships improved as well. Alan and I looked at these moments frame by frame, and that careful inspection led to interesting insights. Alan recognized that in each instance he had taken on more than 100 percent responsibility and had made a clear request to the other individual to change it to 100 percent. The juxtaposition of these two elements (balanced responsibility and making requests) was exciting to him. It gave him much to consider between meetings with me.

As a result of experimenting and thinking of new ways of moving forward, Alan reported that he took some specific action steps:

I began looking over a list of community pro bono projects and seeing what items could possibly be let go as a means of helping me see where I was preventing space for billable client projects. I started thinking about a specific request I could make of the participants in my upcoming workshop at the Chamber of Commerce that would help create a positive call to action that in turn would add value to the clients and connect them back with me for other potential billable work.

Destiny

Once Alan could clearly envision his dream for his business, he went about designing and building that dream. As the coaching relationship drew toward completion, Alan was able to reflect:

To bring this story back to the beginning and to close the loop I've created, let me explain the real-world, tangible outcomes and benefits I've realized as a result of the coaching I received:

- *At the beginning of our coaching sessions, I had only one billable project.*

  Less than three months into the coaching, I had four additional paying clients.

- *At the beginning of our coaching sessions, I had no positive prospects for future billable work.*

  Less than three months into the coaching, I had over a dozen potential future billable clients.

- *At the beginning of our coaching sessions, I was great at networking and marketing, but lousy at closing the sale.*

  Less than three months into the coaching, I was consciously using a real-time economic exchange process that was resulting in the aforementioned contracts and potential clients.

- *At the beginning of our coaching sessions, I was not at all sure I would have any success at selling enough billable work to sustain the business.*

> Less than three months into the coaching, I had already
> sold enough work to sustain the business for the next
> twelve months, and was looking forward to a hugely suc-
> cessful year . . . perhaps the best in the last five years in
> terms of sales and income.

I credit my coach, and her positive questions, with helping me understand more about myself and how to leverage my own natural strengths
and to create more and better possibilities for myself and my business. I
now have a real-time capacity for creating a mutually beneficial economic
exchange that allows both my clients and me to be much more successful. I have a much more positive awareness and much higher energy
around my own strengths, and I know how to leverage them. My vision
is now firmly within my grasp, and tangible results have already occurred.
What can I say? The appreciative approach worked miracles for me.

Alan's coach observes:

His new status as sole proprietor in the business gave Alan the
impetus and power to dream big. It gave him new energy to enter into
areas that were his personal passion. With renewed energy and his
newly discovered skills in marketing and sales, he found opportunity
after opportunity open to him. Using the economic exchange process we
had developed together, Alan was able to ask for payment for his services
where he would have given them away in the past. After three months of
coaching, Alan had booked enough business and was bringing in enough
money to cover all his anticipated expenses for the coming year! We are
now ready to move on to our next cycle of coaching, in which Alan will
create an explicit vision of how he can market and sell the services that
are integral to his business and natural to his style. He is already well on
his way.

Reflection

This story represents the best of what we hope to offer coaches,
potential coaches, and managers who coach. It describes how
Appreciative Coaching works, and we hope that you will come

to share our own passion for Appreciative Inquiry, our core philosophy, and the application of this core philosophy to coaching relationships.

Alan, because of his work in organization development and change, knew more about the work of coaching than most. He knew, as he stated without much enthusiasm, that the most common way to approach change was to address an organization's or individual's weaknesses. This deficit approach has been the most heavily trodden path to personal and professional change. Now, however, there are a wide variety of positive approaches that use strengths, past achievements, and visioning, and suggest that people can change without the frustration of trying to improve things for which they had neither genuine enthusiasm nor unquestioned expertise. The traditional notions of change and development came out of a worldview that people were infinitely perfectible. Change resulted from addressing problems and overcoming resistance gradually, over time. Newer philosophies claim that if people manage their strengths and past accomplishments wisely, they can achieve far greater benefits than if they toil away at incremental improvements to their weaknesses.

Not so long ago, people saw themselves and their world as machinelike; like gears, they had to mesh with other parts to ensure a well-operating whole company or family. Now people see life much more as their own construction, one that incorporates their professional, religious, familial, or cultural background, but does not use that history to put boundaries around what they might be.

The rapid rise of coaching as a profession is a direct response to this desire for self-construction. The proliferation of coaching schools, Internet sites, conferences, and professional associations speaks to the need among new and experienced coaches for networking and education in evidence-based methods. Certification increasingly seeks to bring rigor and consistent quality to coaching. Today there are a multitude of coaching programs, models, and approaches to choose from. Some of them are based on the principles of a problem-solving approach, and some of them incorporate many of the ideas, concepts, and principles that underlie Appreciative Coaching.

The Basic Structure of the Appreciative Approach

The purpose of this book is to offer coaches and clients an engaging and concrete process for change, based not on traditional "fix your weaknesses" methods but on the positive philosophy of Appreciative Inquiry. AI is a powerful, highly successful process for change in the arena of organizational development that has been widely and enthusiastically embraced by corporations, nonprofits, and governmental and nongovernmental organizations worldwide over the past twenty years. We authors apply this well-documented group method to the environment of one-on-one coaching. Inherent in an appreciative approach to change are certain elements that we deal with in detail in different chapters of the book. These include the use of appreciative questions, the five principles of Appreciative Coaching, and the four stages of Appreciative Coaching.

Loving the Questions

One of the fundamental premises of an appreciative approach is the incredible power inherent in asking the "right" questions. These are not just any questions, but questions that are carefully crafted to create a joyfully focused state of mind as the client considers and answers them. Alan noted that even his coach's initial written questions evoked anticipation and enthusiasm. In our own experience, we've noticed how some questions can send us off on a mental magic carpet. These are the questions someone asks us or we ask ourselves that transport us mentally because we are so entranced with the images the questions raise. These grab our attention because our motivation to explore them supersedes whatever is going on in the moment. They do this in a way that a statement or another kind of question does not.

We asked ourselves, Can we think of a recent question that did this for us? Here's an example that engages us every time: "What gives you energy in your life right now?" This question makes us curious about ourselves. It helps us focus on what we most enjoy, get wrapped up in, lose ourselves in, look forward to. We can journal about this or talk to a friend or colleague about it for hours. In contrast, if someone asks us to list the five most important work goals we have for the next year, we know this is important, but the question just doesn't engage us in the same way.

What is it about questions, positive questions, questions that engage people in thinking about their own best selves, that puts them into what psychologist Mihaly Csikszentmihalyi calls "flow"?[2] Poet Rainer Maria Rilke recommended to his younger poet friend that we all embrace these kinds of questions and begin living them without trying to figure out too quickly what the answers might be.[3]

This book is also about loving the questions—not just any questions, but the questions that cause us to say *yes* to life, exploration, and experimentation, and *yes* to change. The appreciative approach assumes that the questions people ask affect the way they think about their past, present, and potential future. We will describe our experience working with this method and offer templates, exercises, and, of course, sample questions, to allow any practicing or potential coaches or managers to incorporate Appreciative Coaching into their existing practice.

The Five Principles of Appreciative Coaching

Underlying the appreciative approach are five basic principles that have been tested and established as the core philosophy for Appreciative Coaching.[4] We present the five principles in greater detail in Chapters Three and Four. For now, we introduce them to set our stage.

Principle One: The Constructionist Principle

The Constructionist Principle posits that knowing and becoming are interwoven. Many believe that as the world gets more and more complex, the relevance of empirical truths diminishes. This implies that there are, in reality, not very many generalizations people can make, or sure predictors of repeatable interactions. However, we are sure that the recognition and acknowledgment of who a person is now and how she became who she is now is a strong predictor of who she can and will become. Furthermore, it is not a matter of fate or predestination. In other words, a person's future is an extension of what she knows and doesn't know, both as coach and as client. A person's actions (what she is doing and has done) contribute to her current reality and put boundaries around what she believes she can be. By inquiring about clients' past successes, we determine what clients know and how we can apply what they know to a desirable future. We can often expand clients' boundaries through our active application of this principle.

As you recall in Alan's story, the coach began working with Alan by methodically inquiring into his abilities, talents, past successes, and unmet desires. She repeatedly questioned him on his perceptions of himself, which resulted in a number of significant insights for him: that he often took more than 100 percent responsibility, that he was more successful in past situations when he made direct requests of others, and that when he combined both 100 percent responsibility with making clear requests of others, things worked very well for him and his clients. Alan began to see that, consciously or not, he was constructing much of the reality he experienced.

Principle Two: The Positive Principle

Positive attitudes, actions, and connections influence long-term change. The more positive all these elements remain, the longer lasting the change will be. The Positive Principle is an overarching principle for our Appreciative Coaching practice. It suggests that when both the coach and the client are connected as partners in the positive pursuit of a dream and when they both retain (mostly) positive attitudes and act toward the change they want, the change will happen positively. It may happen even faster if clients (even

the very negative clients) change in ways that allow them to perceive themselves as effective actors on their own behalf.

The Positive Principle may be the one most obviously present
in all the coaching we do. It is visible in the positive bonding
between Alan and his coach, in Alan's repeated wonder at their
positive conversations in which they built on each other's ideas,
and in Alan's positive affect throughout their formal relationship
together.

Principle Three: The Simultaneity Principle

Inquiry and change happen in the same moment according to
the Simultaneity Principle. To put it another way, the future happens in and as a result of the present. We sow the seeds of change
with the very first questions we ask. The kinds of questions we ask
set change in motion in a particular direction. If our questions are
negative or focused on troubles, the client may defend himself
against change or become depressed at the prospect of marginally
improving weaknesses. Perhaps the mandate is even to improve
weaknesses the client cares little about improving. Careful questions create the foundations for what the coach and client discover,
and those discoveries become the foundations for dreaming and
designing clients' destinies. For coaches and clients, this is often
slow and sometimes painful. Eventually, however, our insistence on
framing stories positively engages clients in their own dreams.

Alan was a client who responded quickly and positively to the
appreciative questions being asked by his coach. Even in completing
the Coaching Prep Forms before the first session, Alan felt as
though he had gotten "an injection of positive vibes." Just asking
him positive questions prompted new thinking and awareness on
his part, so that the inquiry immediately elicited change.

Principle Four: The Poetic Principle

The Poetic Principle suggests that life stories can be rewritten
to better fit how clients see themselves in their present or future.

Any number of new realities can flow from a reinterpretation of one's life story, just as there are any number of potential interpretations of a poem. Not all coaching clients come with positive life stories. The Poetic Principle reminds the coach and client that a story can be reframed, reimagined, and refocused to enable more hopeful and joyful action toward a desired change. For example, Alan's coach helped him see that although his recent experiences with his business growth were not positive, he had the potential to see himself differently in the future.

Principle Five: The Anticipatory Principle

The Anticipatory Principle states that a particular dream of the future can guide current behavior in the direction of that future. Focusing clients on their particular vision or dream enables them to take clearer action in the present toward that dream. The Anticipatory Principle is akin to affirmations that are stated positively in the present and that relate to some desired future state.

In the case of Alan, after helping him discover insights about his past behaviors and current potential, his coach intentionally moved Alan toward talking about a new dream for his business. She knew that recognizing his past successes and identifying his current strengths and abilities were not enough to cause change if Alan had no picture of where he wanted to be.

As Alan's story illustrates, our Appreciative Coaching model (Figure 1.1) begins with the choice of a topic for the coaching relationship and then progresses through four related stages. In Chapters Six through Nine, we feature the stages in greater detail to help you understand the intricacies of the Appreciative Coaching approach. We also share what has happened for us and our clients in each stage, and what our experience and research lead us to anticipate happening for you. For now, a brief introduction to the stages will give you the beginning vocabulary of Appreciative Coaching (AC).

Figure 1.1. The Appreciative Coaching Model

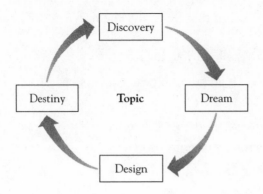

Choosing the Topic

The core process of AC begins with the selection of a topic. In Alan's case, he and his coach agreed that the topic for their coaching would be "making money doing the work he loves." Instead of beginning the coaching relationship with his frustrations that he was "not obtaining enough billable client work to sustain business" or with his "feeling demoralized because he was not able to make an adequate living doing the work he loved," his coach helped Alan reframe his problem into a more positive topic statement.

Much of the language describing the appreciative approach is intentionally positive, or at the very least neutral. This is true of the first word used in every appreciative process, namely, *topic*. For most of us, "topic" means something we'll investigate. It doesn't have effort or possible failure attached to it, as the word *goal* might. At the outset of the coaching relationship, the topic choice is fluid. Core questions explore the client's strengths, her past successes, her work and personal values, and the one or two things she longs to have more of or to have be different in her life. From the answers to these questions come the tools for learning and change.

Stage One: Discovery

In the Discovery Stage, the coach begins exploration by asking specific core questions that move the client in a positive direction:

1. What gives life to you now?
2. Describe a high point or peak experience in your life or work up to now.
3. What do you most value about yourself, your relationships, and the nature of your work?
4. What one or two things do you want more of?

The answers to the questions focus attention on the client's positive history, strengths, and deepest successes. Even when clients come to coaching with a problem to be solved, they may be able to let go of the problem in the Discovery Stage. We saw that this was the case with Alan. He became energized by the positive language and intent and was able to allow his coach to help him explore examples of past successes and current abilities that he could leverage in his current situation. Trust begins to build in the coaching relationship when clients can experience some positive feelings about themselves and their situation.

Stage Two: Dream

In the Dream Stage, client and coach come together to make sense of the answers to the core questions so that they may apply these answers to the topic. When we are in the Dream Stage, we are using the client's proudest accomplishments, core skills and strengths, and deepest values to create something with which we can explore and experiment. Alan could see for himself that there was a disconnect between his current situation and where he truly wanted to be with his business. By taking the time to describe a new vision, Alan felt much more "vibrant and full of possibilities" than he had just a few weeks before. He was able to discuss this with his partner and achieve an amicable separation—something he had thought about but not acted on for over three years.

Stage Three: Design

Once clients bring their dream into clear view, it is time to design a plan for the dream. The Design Stage relates to the ongoing dance between coach and client of defining, performing, and assessing experiments. What might the client do that leads in the direction of the dream? Again the language is deliberate in its positive or neutral emphasis. Design implies a plan or an impression or a mock-up of some future reality. When children play with building blocks, they will often knock down an initial design just for fun. There is no assumption that an initial design is the final design. Experimentation is the order of the day. The ultimate design incorporates as many of the skills and strengths of the client as is possible or appropriate. Over the course of Alan's coaching relationship, once he had identified a new process with which to experiment (the economic exchange process), he began applying his new learnings to marketing and sales. He began to integrate his current insights with what had worked successfully for him in the past. He was literally able to renegotiate with his own clients on the spot when he realized that his work with them was not shared appropriately.

Stage Four: Destiny

Clients step into the Destiny Stage once they have begun to implement the concrete actions and practices they identified and designed in the previous stage for realizing their desired future. The Destiny Stage is a time for clients to acknowledge and celebrate the accomplishments they are making in either moving toward or actually realizing their dream. At the conclusion of this fourth stage, clients usually have two choices: they may signal the successful completion of the coaching relationship, or they may choose to move to a second cycle of Appreciative Coaching by expanding on other elements of their dream or creating a new dream. In either case, it is an opportunity for coaches to help clients reflect on the work they have done and appreciate the results they have achieved.

Alan had no difficulty identifying the real-world, tangible outcomes and benefits he realized from his coaching. He experienced significant increases in billable projects and positive prospects and was looking forward to a very successful year. Although not all clients enjoy such dramatic, positive results, all our coaching research subjects and coaching clients report positive results from engaging in an Appreciative Coaching process. This process of emphasizing the positive seems (in most cases) to generate positive feelings, increased energy, and a deeper connection to oneself. Exploring one's innermost desires turns out to be a pleasurable experience!

Summary

In this chapter, we presented an Appreciative Coaching case study and brought in the perspectives of both the client and the coach as they moved through the four stages of our coaching model. We also briefly introduced the five principles underlying our approach and sought to demonstrate their presence during the different stages. Our intent was to give you a feeling for the basic Appreciative Coaching method that we have found to be so successful.

Subsequent chapters will focus in more detail on the elements of our appreciative approach and will offer a repertoire of tools for your own toolbox. But first, we will give you some of the history and background of four positive methodologies, including AI, that inform the practice of Appreciative Coaching.

2

Positive Methods

You've got to ac-cent-tchu-ate the positive.
Johnny Mercer and Harold Arlen,
"Ac-Cent-Tchu-Ate the Positive," 1944 song

This book is about using coaching to help individuals change. Coaching draws on a rich heritage of individual and organizational change practiced in the fields of organizational behavior, psychology, and psychotherapy. In the last two decades, these fields have gone through major shifts of attention from deficit-based structures and processes to those oriented to well-being and flourishing. Scholars in each field have noted the imbalance of attention and have called for a new examination of the understudied phenomena of positive-based change.

We believe that it is important for future practitioners of Appreciative Coaching to understand the theoretical underpinnings of the practice and to be able to see how appreciative processes and tools relate to the theory. In this chapter, we present the theoretical foundation on which Appreciative Coaching is based, including certain powerful assumptions about human change. Appreciative Coaching uses AI as the basis of its methodology; however, it also draws from the advances made in the arenas of organizational behavior, psychology, and psychotherapy. This chapter reviews the major theoretical underpinnings of Appreciative Coaching from these legacy fields, which inform and enhance each other. We begin with a general description of what is called the "new emerging paradigm" in the physical and social sciences and follow that with a review of the four main bodies of research that underlie our coaching method: AI, Positive Organizational Scholarship, Positive Psychology, and Solution-Focused Brief Therapy.

A New Emerging Paradigm

Each of these four fields of research and practice was born out of what many have referred to as the new emerging paradigm in the physical and social sciences. This new paradigm or world perspective sees life in a fundamentally different way than scientists did in the early twentieth century. Instead of seeing an objective, predictable, and controllable universe, scientists in the twenty-first century see a vastly different world based on the findings of quantum physics and the new sciences of chaos theory, self-organizing systems, and complexity theory.[1] In the traditional worldview, scholars perceived change as incremental, linear, and predictable in terms of simple cause and effect. Now scientists view human and organizational change in the context of complexity, subjectivity, interconnectedness, collaboration, and collective use of language to create social reality. The theories and practices of Appreciative Inquiry, Positive Organizational Scholarship, Positive Psychology, and Solution-Focused Brief Therapy are firmly rooted in this emerging paradigm. We can best understand this paradigm by highlighting one key perspective of this new worldview: social constructionism.

To understand social constructionism, we must ask, What is reality? How do people understand the world? In the traditional paradigm based on the "pure" science of Newtonian thinking, social scientists sought to remain objective and removed from the thing they studied in order to view the world as it is—fixed and predictable. Scientists of the modernist era (the mid-eighteenth century to the late twentieth century) looked for underlying structures and an underlying truth that could be scientifically proven. Post-modern thought, from which social constructionism springs, rejects the notion of static underlying structures and a search for truth in favor of a belief in multiple, contextual realities.[2] Social constructionist theorists point out that humans are different from the physical world. They have language and can therefore interact in symbolic ways. They can "collaborate in the investigation of their own world."[3] With knowledge, humans can change their world. In fact, humans create meaning through their collective dialogue as members of groups, organizations, and societies. The key to the construction of social meaning is language,[4] an important element in the creation of a positive present and future in each of the four practices that inform the foundation of Appreciative Coaching.

Integral to social constructionism and thus to the appreciative approach is the notion of individuals as active, independent, and spontaneous beings who, consciously or not, form images of the future toward which they then grow. This exciting finding is at the core of some major psychological theories that now support a new science of human strength and resilience. Dominant theories of the past viewed the individual primarily as a passive vessel capable only of responding to stimuli. But according to Positive Psychology theorists Seligman and Csikszentmihalyi, individuals are decision makers with choices, preferences, and the possibility of becoming masterful in their own lives.[5] Cooperrider agrees: "to a far greater extent than is normally acknowledged, we human beings create our own realities through symbolic and mental processes."[6]

Appreciative Inquiry: A Revolutionary Force

AI has become a force to be reckoned with in the arena of positive group and organizational change. It has swept not only the nation but also the globe with many examples of its successful applications. There is now a worldwide portal devoted to this rapidly growing discipline, Appreciative Inquiry Commons (http://appreciativeinquiry.case.edu), which functions as a clearinghouse for the sharing of academic resources and practical tools and which includes an annotated bibliography of more than five hundred publications on Appreciative Inquiry and positive change. These publications represent worldwide AI efforts on every continent and discuss applications in a wide variety of fields and organizational settings, including health care, education, religion, and government.

Since the appearance of AI twenty years ago, researchers and practitioners have described it in many ways. It has been called a philosophy, a revolutionizing force, a transformational change process, a life-giving theory and practice, and even a new worldview.[7] Participants in AI initiatives call it "a hopeful and radical shift" in how complex human organizations can achieve sustainable and transformative change.[8] What has caused such excitement and passion? The best answer is that AI just seems to work. It seems to satisfy the hunger so many people have to create meaningful work lives that are both life affirming and inspirational.

David Cooperrider developed AI with other graduate students at Case Western Reserve University because he found problem solving to be an overused method for effecting change in organizations.[9] He searched for a way to shift the prevailing strategy away from fixing problems that might or might not make an organization better toward discovering what individuals and businesses wanted their organizations to be. Cooperrider and his colleagues could not have anticipated that AI would introduce such a major shift in the practice of organizational change. Instead of focusing on what was not working, they began exploring what gave life to people and their workplaces when they were at their very best. They dared to ask questions about hope and inspiration and began to see that organizations were not problems to be solved but miracles and mysteries to be appreciated.

How do we create the future? Is it an extension of the past and nothing more? What is the relationship between a positive image and positive action? Questions like these have generated a vast literature of research studies in the social sciences. In 1990, Cooper-rider wrote a groundbreaking article about positive change in organizations; he referred to positive effects that ranged from the placebo effect in medicine to the Pygmalion studies, and to the importance of positive emotions in human development and emotional health—all supporting the power of positive imagery.[10] His conclusion was that human systems show a remarkable tendency to move toward positive images of the future that those systems themselves have created.

AI is defined as an approach to organizational analysis and learning that is intended for discovering, understanding, and fostering innovation. Its practitioners find that it is "life affirming" and that four propositions underlie its practice:[11]

1. Inquiry should begin with appreciation.

2. Inquiry into what is possible should yield information that can be used, applied, and validated in action.

3. Knowledge that appreciates "what is" becomes provocative and can stir organization members to action.

4. Inquiry into human potential should be collaborative, assuming an immutable relationship between the process of inquiry and its content.

In essence, "AI is a form of organizational study that selectively seeks to locate, highlight, and illuminate what are referred to as the 'life-giving' forces of the organization's existence, its *positive core*."[12]

Also inherent in AI are assumptions about life, people, and the process of change itself. As we have noted, theorists and practitioners of AI have conducted extensive research over the years to build a strong foundation for the AI approach. This foundation includes some common basic assumptions,[13] which seem revolutionary in comparison to the early modernist notions of an objective, predictable, and controllable universe. These same AI assumptions, with minor adaptations (italicized here), form the basis of our model of Appreciative Coaching:

- In every society, organization, group, *or individual*, something works.

- What people focus on becomes their reality.

- Reality is created in the moment, and there are multiple realities.

- The act of asking questions of an organization, group, *or individual* influences the group *or individual* in some way.

- People are more confident and comfortable in their journey to the future (the unknown) when they carry forward parts of the past (the known).

- If people carry parts of the past forward, those parts should be what is best about the past.

- It is important to value differences.

- The language people use creates their reality.

Like AI, Appreciative Coaching is both a theory and practice of change from a holistic framework, but its primary focus is on individuals. Like AI, Appreciative Coaching holds the same core set of assumptions or beliefs: in essence, that human systems (and therefore, individuals) will move toward the "generative and creative images that reside in their most positive core—their values, visions, achievements, and best practices."[14]

Positive Organizational Scholarship

Positive Organizational Scholarship (POS) is a parallel pursuit to AI. Founded in the early 1990s by Kim Cameron, Jane Dutton, and Robert Quinn of the Stephen M. Ross School of Business at the

University of Michigan, it is not a single theory at all, but a discipline that promotes an interest in positive attributes and dynamics in organizations. Like AI, POS investigates the positive. It systematically investigates what makes life worth living, by observing and examining positive phenomena within organizations as well as positive organizational processes. Also like AI, POS neither ignores nor dismisses the negative states in many organizations, but chooses to focus on areas where traditional organizational studies have given less emphasis. POS examines the elements in organizations that help develop strengths, foster resiliency, and produce extraordinary performance. Its researchers ask us to imagine organizations that are characterized by trustworthiness, resilience, wisdom, humility, and high levels of positive energy.[15] Although the human interest of POS is primarily in organizational processes and relationships, researchers also pay significant attention to the individual within organizations, studying such topics as developing authentic leadership,[16] finding positive meaning at work,[17] and forming high-quality connections.[18]

Although today's organizations, particularly large ones, are sometimes bureaucracies that protect the status quo and constrain unusual action, people within them do take "courageous, principled action" for change.[19] The developers of POS found that the nature of the action people take depends to some degree on their organization's structure. But there is no indication that organizational structure entirely constrains people from displaying courage and principles in their action taking. Positive politics, or creating positive connections and networking within and across organizations, also affect one's ability to enjoy work and be effective in organizations.

Because most of our coaching clients live within such organizational systems as corporations, nonprofits, religious and academic institutions, and families, POS becomes relevant to our model of Appreciative Coaching. We acknowledge that some environments are positive for our clients and can nurture change, whereas others are toxic or discouraging to our clients in some way. When our clients are in challenging circumstances, we can encourage them to reframe their experiences in a more positive way or to experiment with changing their environment. When our clients come to us with a leadership vision, POS's description of the best of connecting and networking adds to our ability to help them envision effective leadership. We can also use the focus of POS to help us design experiments with our coaching clients to increase the quality and breadth of their networks.

In Appreciative Coaching, we draw on the work of POS to help our clients identify positive elements of their organization that enable or support their most successful actions. We help them experiment with actions most likely to lead to their own desired destiny within the given constraints of their organizations. The work in POS suggests that particular Appreciative Coaching strategies can help our clients be most effective in taking courageous, principled action.

Positive Psychology

The field of psychology has made its own shift in focus from the study of pathology to the study of conditions and processes that contribute to flourishing or optimal functioning. At the outset of his tenure as president of the American Psychological Association in 1998, Martin Seligman saw the need for a new focus in psychology. Like his colleagues in organizational behavior, he saw in psychology an emphasis on sickness and disease, with little attention being paid to what created energy and joy for people. He described the focus of psychology as getting people from a negative state to zero, with little attention paid to what might get them to a plus five! He began to speak and write with colleagues about the elements of what he came to call Positive Psychology (PP).

The time was right for this shift of attention. Its advent was marked by the January 2000 issue of *American Psychologist*, which was entirely dedicated to this new focus. Seligman and Mihaly Csikszentmihalyi wrote the editorial article introducing the field and a few of its prominent scholars.[20] They noted that psychologists knew quite a lot about how people survive and endure adversity, but had scant knowledge about what makes life worth living. They traced the field's historical roots and noted that prior to World War II, the mission of psychology was threefold: curing mental illness, making the lives of all people more productive and fulfilling, and identifying and nurturing high talent. After World War II, psychology lost its focus on the second two areas. Even humanistic psychology of the 1960s, which launched the self-help movement, never established an empirical base of research which might have attracted the attention of scholars in the field.

In their article, Seligman and Csikszentmihalyi shared their conviction that "the time is finally right for positive psychology"[21] and reminded colleagues that "psychology is not just the study of pathology, weakness, and damage; it is also the study of strength and virtue."[22] They called for practitioners to recognize that some of the best work they already did was in helping clients amplify strengths rather than repair weaknesses. They predicted that the new view of humans as masters of their own lives would reorient psychology back to the neglected aspects of its mission. Seligman and Csikszentmihalyi recognized that PP was not a new idea and made no claim to originality. They claimed only that the early writers had failed to attract a cumulative, empirical body of research to ground their ideas.

Although he began his career with a negative orientation (referring to himself as a dyed-in-the-wool pessimist), Seligman came to believe that people can be happy about the past, happy in the present, and hopeful about the future, though not necessarily all at the same time. Ideally a person's happiness can become pervasive if she were to reframe her narrative about an unhappy past, a dissatisfying present, or a hopeless future. Seligman thought that if people make more conscious use of what he calls "signature strengths"—those unique skills and abilities that individuals express easily—they can be happier in an authentic way.[23] He believed that all emotions about the past are generated by thought and interpretation, and that people can reimagine or rethink past unhappy experiences in such a way that they can become genuinely happier about them.[24] To achieve or retain authentic happiness (our greatest state of well-being), Seligman believed that people must use their individual and unique strengths both to enrich their own experience and to make a contribution to others in relationships and organizations.

Many others have made great contributions to PP. Edward Diener, working with Seligman, found that the enduring conditions that enable happiness are friends, faith, and family.[25] Kahneman researched and emphasized the experiencing self—that is, the self that experiences happiness in the moment—whether the person is reading a good book or celebrating a birthday.[26] This happiness is more ephemeral and has three main components: pleasure for anything, from a good meal to a warm bed; engagement with friends, work, or romance; and meaning—that is, using one's strengths and discipline to make the world better in some way. Csikszentmihalyi had in a sense anticipated the work in PP with his own work related to the experience of flow,[27] the loss of self-consciousness and the evaporation of time that occurs when an individual is deeply involved with some passionate activity. Daniel Goleman, in his work with emotional intelligence (EQ),[28] described well-being in our professional interactions with others.

PP has enticed researchers from other fields to enter into the examination of positive phenomena. Social psychologists and sociologists who study the psychology of relationships and groups have made significant contributions. The research of the Gallup organization, resulting in the books *How Full is Your Bucket?* by Rath and Clifton, and *First, Break all the Rules,* by Buckingham and Coffman, indicates that people perform better and are happier at work when they use primarily their strengths. Continuing from this work, Clifton developed the StrengthsFinder Profile (available at www.strengthsfinder.com) to help individuals identify their talents so that they can build them into strengths and enjoy consistent, near-perfect performance.

Other contributors include collaborators Wilson, Gilbert, Loewenstein, and the aforementioned Kahneman.[29] This group of psychologists and economists currently write about happiness and satisfaction and the decision-making process that shapes people's sense of well-being. They have shown that people do not, for the most part, become happy or satisfied in the ways that they think they do. People base their decisions to do things they suppose will make them happy, such as buying a new car or having children, on the emotional consequences they think they will experience. But it turns out that they are almost always wrong. These researchers have observed, over and over again, that humans are not very good at forecasting their feelings and, as a result, are not necessarily adept at improving their well-being. What people tend to do is overestimate both the intensity and the duration of their feelings, both positive and negative. Gilbert said that the problem is not that a person can't always get what she wants, but that she can't always know what she wants.[30] Wilson suggested that people could better forecast their feelings by "vividly" imagining a future situation and attending to how that situation would make them feel. This "sampling" of future feelings may forecast the motivations and attitudes that will be concurrent with the actual event.[31]

As Appreciative Coaches, we are reminded by these researchers to test what clients say they want against their experiments and behavior in the present. Our clients can find what they want by reflecting on each of their experiments, by determining the strength and duration of their satisfaction and enjoyment, and by building on their enjoyment of particularly meaningful experiences.

PP informs practitioners of Appreciative Coaching of the workings of the human mind, emotions, and spirit. This research gives us direction in how to support our clients in their growth, both when our clients are in a state of positive expectation and when they are not. PP moves us beyond the formulation of problems and their resolutions; it helps us understand as coaches what happiness is and how we can guide our clients to use their strengths to achieve their deepest desires.

Solution-Focused Brief Therapy

The Brief Therapy model arose from family psychotherapy. First developed in the late 1960s by Weakland and others, Brief Therapy practitioners contend that "the beliefs and theories held by a therapist may strongly influence not only his technique but also the length and outcome of his treatments."[32] The model is founded on two points of the renowned psychoanalytic and personality theorist Milton Erikson. First, the aim of the therapist is not to clarify the reality of a situation but to better it in some way. Second, the therapist accepts what the client has to offer and turns it to positive use, even if it appears as resistance or pathology. The Brief Therapy approach does not delve into understanding the roots or patterns of a problem; that is, the *why* of a problem is not relevant. Rather, the therapy seeks to resolve problems by helping the client substitute behaviors that will break undesired patterns. This therapy is called brief, not because of an emphasis on expediency or a goal, but because of its premises about the nature and handling of psychiatric problems.[33]

This pragmatic approach captured the interest of Insoo Kim Berg and Steve de Shazer, who became the leading proponents and developers of the model known as Solution-Focused Brief Therapy (SFBT).[34] Their model differs in two significant ways from the widely used problem-solving approach generally applied in the field of psychotherapy. First, the premise of SFBT is that the future is created and negotiated. Therefore, an individual is not considered a slave of past experiences, not even of traumatic or life-altering events, but can learn to negotiate and implement many useful steps leading to a more satisfying life. Although during SFBT an individual's problems and history are not explored in detail, the therapist does attempt, in a nonblaming and nonpathologizing way, to acknowledge the challenge facing the person and its resulting distress.[35] The second distinction rests in the SFBT belief that a small change can lead to big differences in the future; that is, change in one part of the system can effect change in the whole system. Described as a minimalist approach and fitting within the theory of social constructionism, SFBT pays great attention to the use of language, its practitioners believing that language shapes the perception of reality.

In practice, the task of brief therapy is to help clients do something different and achieve a solution by changing their behavior or their interpretations of behavior and the situation. Without needing the details of the complaint, the client and therapist answer the question, How will we know when the problem is solved? The aim is to start the solution process rather than to stop the complaint pattern. The therapist supports this process by complimenting the client on what he is already doing that is useful or good in some way. The compliments are designed to help the client reframe, to see situations in a more flexible way, and to give the message that the therapist sees things the client's way and agrees. Practitioners follow this formula: "If it works, do more of it. If it doesn't work, don't do it again, do something else."[36] They firmly believe that if clients "have survived this far in their lives, they surely know how to go a little further. Most clients have abilities but they do not believe they do."[37]

Many SFBT techniques are widely used today in numerous settings with a variety of populations and problems. Three of these techniques are its hallmark. The first, asking questions that elicit exceptions to problems, helps clients acknowledge times when a difficulty is absent, easier to cope with, or less pervasive. Rather than asking whether there is an exception, the therapist asks questions in a manner implying that there is always an exception to be remembered. The identification of exceptions shifts the focus from the problem to possible remedies or solutions.

The second technique, the miracle question, was designed as a way to help clients describe a picture of their preferred future. The question is carefully crafted to fire the imagination of the client and is usually asked in this way: "Suppose that tonight, while you are

sleeping, a miracle happens and the problem that has been trou-
bling you sorts itself out overnight . . . what would you see the next
morning that would let you know the miracle had happened? What
would you find yourself doing the day after the miracle, what would
others notice you doing?"[38] Responses to the miracle question may
not represent well-formed, realistic goals; rather, they help point
the way to a desired future.

The third technique is the use of scaling questions as a way to
help move a client closer toward a goal. Anything can be scaled.
The therapist might ask, for example, "On a scale of 1 to 10, where
1 represents how badly you felt when you first came to see me and 10
represents how you will feel when you no longer need to see me,
where are you today?" Most often the client's response is a number
in the middle of the scale, which allows the therapist to follow with
a question that explores the positive things the client is doing that
allowed her to reach the number she identified.

In the SFBT model, the therapist works to identify clues (suggestions, tasks, directives, and so on) for action the client might
take that will be good for him and lead him toward a solution. Practitioners firmly believe that "what you expect to happen influences
what you do."[39] Berg asserts that the most respectful way to work
with clients is to encourage them to feel a sense of control over what
happens to them, and to encourage making choices. This approach
prevents others' having to lower themselves to a defensive position yet holds them accountable in the most respectful, empowering way.[40]

Because the core belief that "a positive focus will support positive outcomes" underlies both SFBT and Appreciative Coaching,
it is perhaps not surprising that Brief Therapy techniques work well
with the Appreciative Coaching method. In fact, you will find that
Appreciative Coaching uses questions about exceptions and questions about an imagined miracle. The scaling questions and other
SFBT techniques are easily carried over as well. Although most
coaching methods are brief compared to traditional therapy, we

have found this therapeutic tradition most friendly to our positive, appreciative approach.[41]

Summary

This chapter presented the major theories underlying Appreciative Coaching. We began by describing the new sciences and social constructionism as key elements in four bodies of research that inform our work: Appreciative Inquiry, Positive Organizational Scholarship, Positive Psychology, and Solution-Focused Brief Therapy. We discussed the shift in focus that these fields represent—from deficit-based theories to those of human well-being and flourishing. AI, POS, PP, and SFBT each arose from the recognition of an imbalance. Leaders in each field called for the redirection of attention so that researchers, practitioners, and clients would focus on the best in life. These leaders all claim that their fields have made significant strides in finding alternative ways to address difficult problems and issues. All of these fields focus attention away from problems and toward solutions. Furthermore, scholars in these fields affirm that positive is not simply the absence of negative: positive phenomena deserve to be studied in their own right.

Appreciative Coaching grounds its pursuit in these legacy disciplines. Like the researchers in each of these fields, we do not deny the existence of unpleasant or negative aspects of life, nor do we want to see them through rose-colored glasses.[42] We believe that the positive approaches to learning and change, with particular emphasis on the methods described in AI, offer coaching clients a different way to explore their own deepest longings for well-being at work, in their families, and in their most passionate pursuits.

In our next two chapters, we present each of the five principles in further detail, in particular taking care to present stories, strategies, and language to help Appreciative Coaches recognize what the principles mean in actual practice.

3

The Foundation of Appreciative Coaching—Part I

The Constructionist Principle and the Positive Principle

If you have built castles in the air, your work need not be lost; that is where they should be. Now put foundations under them.

Henry David Thoreau (1817–1862),
American philosopher and naturalist

So far, we have introduced you to the idea and process of Appreciative Coaching and have described the theoretical roots of our approach. But we have not yet explored in depth the beliefs in human potential that form the foundation of Appreciative Coaching. The core assumptions of AI mentioned in the previous chapter are deeply embedded in what practitioners like to call the "DNA of AI," and they are grounded in three main theoretical and research foundations, which we have already touched on: social constructionism, the new sciences, and research on the power of image and positive emotions.

A fundamental link in this DNA is the interplay of five clearly defined principles that help guide AI practitioners in their focus on an appreciative approach (and away from problem solving).[1] These principles shape the philosophy that underlies AI and therefore Appreciative Coaching:

1. Constructionist Principle

2. Positive Principle

3. Simultaneity Principle

4. Poetic Principle

5. Anticipatory Principle

To understand the role of the five principles, imagine the craft involved in weaving beautiful handmade rugs. The foundation of each handwoven rug is made up of threads that run the length (warp) of the loom. They form the base on which the horizontal threads (wefts) are then interwoven. For the weaver to move the weft threads across the loom, the warp threads must be strong and resilient enough to hold the weft in place. The five principles are like the warp threads on the loom: they are philosophically resilient enough to form the base on which the Appreciative Coaching stages unfold, and they inspire the processes and tools that guide us to maintain the integrity of the appreciative approach. They also help identify the distinctions between Appreciative Coaching and other coaching methodologies.

The Principles in Action

We've all had the experience of wanting to help someone else fix or solve her problem or situation. For example, Colleen was struggling with her ability to play volleyball at the varsity level. In general, she described herself as "just a bad player" compared to the other girls and she felt that she wasn't contributing anything to the team. A part of her wanted to quit because she was scared; varsity volleyball was hard, and she didn't know if she could do it. Another part of her wanted to try. It was one of those life lessons that was daunting to a teenager struggling with her belief in herself and her abilities, and daunting to her parents, who wanted to see their child realize her potential.

This dilemma can't be "solved," because contained within it is the evolving mystery of life. Who can predict the right outcome? On the one hand, quitting may lead Colleen to a deepening sense of negativity about herself, or it may be a catalyst for her to try harder at something else. On the other hand, if she does not quit, she might learn that she can achieve her goals despite initial setbacks and disappointments. Reality is created in the moment, and people are usually presented with multiple paths. What about the language Colleen used to describe herself—did that really represent reality as others saw her? Did she have a balanced picture of herself?

In coaching, we interact daily with clients who face their own dilemmas and who also create their own interpretation of those situations. How do we best guide our clients in moving forward without limiting their options or taking away the opportunity for self-discovery? We've found the five principles to be reassuring touchstones with which to monitor and guide our work with clients. The principles may be evident in any of the four coaching stages (Discovery, Dream, Design, and Destiny). In later chapters, as we discuss each stage, we will make references to the principles that seem most commonly to underlie them. Although we have built the foundation of our Appreciative Coaching approach on the five principles of AI, we have also extended and adapted their meaning and application to reflect our specific learnings and experience as Appreciative Coaches and researchers.

We have found that the Constructionist Principle (social knowledge and destiny are intertwined) functions much as it does in the practice of AI, but perhaps at a heightened level because of the one-on-one relationship between a coach and a client. We know that each coaching session can be fateful in guiding clients to learn and understand what is best about themselves. With the Positive Principle (people move in the direction of what they study), AI experience in organizations has shown the need for building and sustaining as much positive affect and social bonding as possible. We have found this to be equally effective in our coaching experiences. We have learned to trust that the appreciative approach generates positive feelings with clients. And from Positive Psychology, we have learned how important it is not only to support the expression of positive emotions in our clients but also to understand the impact our positive affect can have on their affirmative response to change—emotions are indeed contagious! Finally, we have applied concepts from Positive Organizational Scholarship to help clients sustain positive connections and to help them reflect on and appreciate when they are at their personal best.

We found an underlying theme among the Simultaneity, Poetic, and Anticipatory Principles as we applied them to Appreciative Coaching. Although they function similarly to the principles in AI, they bring an added dimension to individual change through their present and future orientation to time. In other words, we have observed that a coach's own perspective of the role time plays in individual change can have an impact on the direction of the coaching strategy. For example, if the coach believes that the pace and scope of individual change is determined primarily by past experiences, she will focus attention on the past and its effect on the client's present and future. If the coach considers the client's beliefs and expectations about his present and future to be as significant as those of the past in the impact on his individual change, she will focus more attention on the possibilities inherent in these beliefs and expectations.

In this chapter, we present the Constructionist and Positive Principles, as they form the core of an appreciative approach. In the next chapter, we talk about the importance of the shared perception of time and change that underlies the Simultaneity, Poetic, and Anticipatory Principles.

The Constructionist Principle

We don't see things as they are, we see them as we are.
Anaïs Nin (1903–1977), French author

As implied by its name, the Constructionist Principle is an expression of the social constructionist understanding of how we as humans view the world. It indicates that theorists and practitioners are moving from a fixed, seemingly objective idea of the capacities of our human potential to a more open exploration of possibilities. Constructionist theory is an approach to human science and practice that "replaces the individual with the *relationship* as the locus of knowledge."[2] This means that how we humans communicate, interact, create symbols, and construct metaphors with one another creates our reality. While we may be able to define the physical world in objective terms, our social and psychic worlds are subjective; that is, we create meaning and reality through human communication and language.[3]

The social constructionist view is equally liberating in Appreciative Coaching. When a person understands that her language and metaphors actually create her reality, she can use this as a catalyst for personal and professional change. If the individual truly doesn't believe that her life is predestined, she can mold and change it with her thoughts and imagination. This is not an easy concept for some clients to embrace, but those willing to try may find change far easier than they had imagined.

Appreciative Coaching is not the only coaching approach to incorporate constructionist theory. Indeed, one of the core tenets of the entire coaching profession is the belief in the ability of clients to recreate themselves and in the importance of language in making that happen. What makes Appreciative Coaching unique is how this belief permeates all aspects of its practice and tools. Three of the assumptions underlying AI are fundamental to this principle: (1) what people focus on becomes their reality; (2) the language people use creates their reality; and (3) in every individual, something works. Therefore, what people know about themselves and how they know it is fateful or full of destiny because these are the only ways individuals know how to understand and relate to themselves, their past, and their potential for the future.[4] In other words, knowing (their strengths, abilities, dreams, and desires) is at the center of every attempt people make at change. Knowing what is best about themselves gives people the base to be able to change in a positive, life-enhancing way.

Recognizing the Constructionist Principle

As Appreciative Coaches, we can do much to guide clients toward a better knowing of themselves. We do this by

- Inquiring into clients' talents, past and present successes, and unmet desires

- Listening for words, phrases, or metaphors that will guide clients toward the reality they seek

- Helping clients create a more holistic and balanced view of themselves

- Gently moving clients from problem language to discovery and appreciative language

- Helping clients create a clear image of the key attributes that they want to keep and build on for the future

- Encouraging clients to take personal responsibility for what they know and how they know it

Because a person's self-awareness and destiny are interwoven,[5] an important part of Appreciative Coaching is the examination of who the client is now and how he talks about himself in the past and present. It's all about what the client pays attention to and is curious about. This then forms the foundation for how he takes action in creating his future.

Kathy's Story

Kathy, a sales representative in a national financial services company, began coaching with a clear desire to build her client base so that she could become fiscally stable herself. She was separated from her husband and had two small children, so she also wished for a happy and stable environment for her girls while she tried to grow a thriving business. She wasn't sure how she could do both without great cost to herself. She had doubts and concerns, but she also had a dream.

Kathy was referred to her coach by the regional director of the company she represented. The director saw potential in Kathy if only she could tap into her latent strengths and believe that she could achieve what she really wanted. Kathy couldn't quite imagine that she could be a leader in the company. She wanted to be a leader—it just seemed to be beyond her reach. Looking at Kathy's past actions and successes, however, her coach knew that Kathy had the potential. She had the strength to get a college education, leave an unfulfilling marriage, and start her own business, then in its second year and holding its own.

Kathy was one of those clients who was willing, with support, to realize that she could in fact create and change her life by altering her thinking and daring to have a dream. Her coach reminded Kathy of her past successes and her current strengths and abilities when she doubted them. Kathy's coach helped her use positive language to override her negative self-talk. They discussed "pivoting"—when Kathy found herself thinking of what she didn't want, she had to stop and ask herself what she really wanted in that situation. They worked continuously on clarifying Kathy's dream.

Partway through the coaching, Kathy created a theme for herself for the year: "leadership and growth within my business and myself." She began creating opportunities to be more proactive in how she interacted with those around her, and started a ten-year plan for herself. She then took the big step (for her) of approaching the regional director about leadership opportunities available to her. Toward the end of her six-month coaching contract, Kathy was tapped by the regional director to attend the company's "Fastrack Academy" for leaders. Kathy informed her coach a few months later that she had qualified for the company's Silver Award and had been recognized at the annual meeting. After attending the academy, Kathy commented to her coach, "It was one of the best experiences of my life, and you helped me get there! I now have to continue with breakthrough projects like we did, and so far, so good!"

As coaches, we continue to be amazed at the power of the constructionist assumptions that underlie Appreciative Coaching: helping clients realize that something about them works (that is, they are already successes), that what they focus on becomes their reality, and that they can alter their reality by the language they choose to use.

Appreciative Language

We have built the Constructionist Principle into our first contact with clients through our Client Information Form (see Appendix B). We use appreciative questions to help clients begin to think about their past and current successes and what they would like to enhance. Here are some sample questions:

- Describe your three greatest accomplishments to date.

- What made these accomplishments stand out for you?

- What have you incorporated into your current actions from your past accomplishments?

- How could you use what you've learned from these accomplishments to assist you in making future changes?

- List five adjectives that describe you at your best.

- What situations tend to bring out your best?

- What are you learning and accepting about yourself at present?

Appreciative language is crucial in helping clients free themselves from outmoded habits and old beliefs. As they begin to understand how their own language and actions have focused their reality in specific ways, they will shift to new words and metaphors to describe where they are and where they want to go. As appreciative coaches, we are catalysts for this type of change through our modeling of language that supports the constructionist belief that people can create and change their life through their thinking and imagining. Table 3.1 is a sampling of appreciative language we found rooted in the Constructionist Principle.[6]

Table 3.1. Examples of Appreciative Language Rooted in the Constructionist Principle

Client Language	Coach Language
And that's when I just stood back and said . . .	How do you talk to yourself about . . .?
I am allowing myself . . .	How do you talk to others about . . .?
I am learning . . .	What words do you associate with . . .?
I am really finished with . . .	
I am willing . . .	This is time for you to be able to reflect on . . .
I don't want to live like this. What do I need to do?	What gives you that spark of life?
Then all of a sudden, I realized . . .	Tell me what worked in the past.
I have begun to realize . . .	Tell me what would engage you.
I have to create some space.	When are you at your best in . . .?
I really started paying attention.	I just want to pick up on something you said about yourself.
I see what the possibilities are.	
I'm eager now.	What does it look like when you . . .?
I'm letting go of some of this stuff.	It sounds like it's related to something you said before.
I'm making a conscious effort to . . .	How can you help yourself . . .?
I'm really noticing it.	So you want a different conversation to happen?
	How did you discover that?
	What if we say that differently?
	I wonder if you thought about . . .?

The Positive Principle

> *There are only two ways to live your life. One is as though nothing is a miracle. The other is as though everything is.*
>
> *Albert Einstein (1879–1955),*
> *theoretical physicist, Nobel laureate*

In our practices, we often find that clients hesitate to claim their own best talents and abilities. Mary, a highly successful manager in a computer company, was very uncomfortable answering some of the appreciative questions about herself. She couldn't come up with five adjectives to describe herself at her best because she did not want to see herself as a braggart. Debra, a mother seeking employment in a depressed economic area, had the same reaction—she would just be bragging if she talked about her strengths. Michelle, head of the local chamber of commerce, reacted negatively when her coach pointed out the awesome opportunity Michelle had to be a catalyst for change in her community. Her immediate response was to feel depressed! Joe, an engineer at a major auto manufacturer, was exploring postretirement options. His coach suggested that he use an appreciative process to ask some close colleagues and friends to help him identify his signature skills and abilities. He was reluctant to do it; he felt uncomfortable asking people about his strengths. Some researchers would say that these individuals are reacting with "norms of humility" that constrain them from acknowledging or asking others to identify their own sources of strength.[7]

Some theorists believe that human beings are wired innately with certain emotions (anger and fear) that compel them to act in particular ways, as evidenced by fight-or-flight reactions.[8] In fact, research on emotions in general has tended to focus mostly on the negative feelings (again, anger and fear) because of the confirmed link between emotions, thoughts, and physiological changes in the body. For example, when human beings feel physically threatened, their bodies react by increasing blood flow to their large muscles. They can then use these muscles to run away or to stay and fight. Traditional research focused on the negative, and neglected positive emotions, such as joy, interest, contentment, and love.[9] Small wonder that many people have not felt encouraged to believe in their own inner strengths. Martin Seligman, the founder of Positive Psychology, summed it up in noting that the pervasive view of human nature, recurring across many cultures, has been the "rotten-to-the-core dogma."[10]

But there is good news! Despite a bias toward problem solving in organizations,[11] fifty years of studying human deficits (mental illness),[12] and a tradition of research favoring the study of negative emotions over positive ones,[13] the tide has finally turned. As we noted in Chapter Two, there is now significant research in such areas as AI, positive emotions, and positive organizations that is effectively demonstrating the power of the positive in creating meaningful, happy lives. As practitioners of Appreciative Coaching, we draw strongly on this growing positive paradigm to further support the Positive Principle as a key foundation of our coaching model.

The Significance of Being Positive

Our definition of the Positive Principle is drawn from AI practitioners' years of experience,[14] from the award-winning research by Barbara Fredrickson on the function of positive emotions,[15] and from studies of how individuals reflect and incorporate positive experiences into a best-self construct.[16] The Positive Principle is an expression of all the concrete ways we can ensure that our coaching clients experience maximally positive effects from the coaching relationship. We achieve this by using positive inquiry and positive emotions and by helping our clients reflect on when they are at their best.

As we've discussed, there is a new focus on the power of the positive. We know, for example, that emotions (both positive and negative) appear to be contagious.[17] Mimicry and feedback play an important role.[18] The perception of an emotional expression can cause the viewer to mimic elements of the expression and to experience the associated feeling(s). That is, the viewer of the emotional expression doesn't just sense the emotion in the other person; she herself may feel and express that emotion to some degree. This mimicking begins early. Newborns seem to know what others are feeling and respond congruently, suggesting that emotions may follow facial expressions and not the other way around. Studies by Fredrickson and others show that positive emotions can be antidotes and even undo the effects of negative emotions. In organizations, the positive emotions of employees and especially of leaders are considered to be especially contagious.[19]

Fredrickson's new model of emotions proposes a different perspective on the role of positive emotions in human evolution. Traditional social science has tended to focus on negative emotions
that are directly linked to urges to act. For example, anger triggers
physiological changes and an urge toward taking specific actions
(for example, raising one's fists). Theorists considered negative emotions as necessary for human survival in crisis situations. Positive
emotions, in contrast, seem diffuse. They do not arise out of life-
threatening situations and therefore do not trigger clear responses
like fight or flight. Instead, they seem to produce a kind of "pleasant subjective feel."[20] In building a new model for positive emotions, Fredrickson found that such feelings as joy, interest,
contentment, and love can be transformational by contributing to
the expansion of a person's ways of thinking and acting.

Fredrickson focused on four positive emotions to demonstrate
her model.[21] *Joy or happiness* creates the urge to be playful. Play
involves exploration and invention. Although play can sometimes
appear to be aimless, it also promotes the acquisition of skills. When
someone is in a joyful state, his mental abilities are sharper, and he
is more willing to try new things. Over time, joy can contribute to
the increase of a person's physical, intellectual, and social skills.
Long after the feeling has passed, the skills remain.

Interest (curiosity, intrigue, excitement, or wonder) is closely
aligned with challenge and intrinsic motivation. When interest
matches what a person perceives to be her skills, she can enjoy a
sense of flow in her life. Interest sparks a person's desire to explore,
to increase her knowledge, and to discover new things. Through
this interest and exploration, she adds to her store of knowledge and
becomes more capable. Interest can be a prime mover of personal
growth, creative endeavor, and enhancement of intelligence.

Contentment (tranquility or serenity) arises in situations where
a person feels safe, such that he expends little effort to assert himself and has a high degree of certainty. This emotion prompts a person to savor his current circumstances and recent successes and to

feel at one with the world. During these moments it is possible for someone to integrate recent past events and achievements into his concept of himself or into his worldview. The effect is to increase the person's resources to take new actions (which in turn lead to new possibilities).

Finally, most theorists consider *love* to be a constellation of emotions that can incorporate joy, interest, and contentment. The essential component of love is its object—other people. Interactions laced with love help build and strengthen social connections and attachments. In lasting relationships, bonds of love deepen and individuals reveal hidden aspects of themselves. As they become increasingly familiar with each other, they feel joy or contentment in an ever deepening cycle. Having once experienced love, individuals can draw on that experience in other relationships; it builds their social resources to be used at a later time.

Fredrickson's model of positive emotions is based on what she identifies as *thought-action tendencies*,[22] which represent a profound difference in how researchers view emotions. Positive emotions, instead of narrowing the thought-action repertoire (as happens with negative emotions, such as those related to fight or flight), actually *broaden* the momentary thought-action repertoire. They allow a person to turn away from automatic (everyday) patterns of behavior and pursue novel, creative, and often unscripted paths of thought and action.

When people are in a positive mode, they act more effectively in their lives.[23] Typically, they are more creative, more motivated to act toward high performance, and more helpful toward others. When they experience positive emotions, people are more alert, and their cognitive ability is sharper. With this increased ability they are able to create more unusual and varied possibilities for action. Positive emotions broaden people's attention and their intellectual and social resources. When a person feels good about herself, she not only feels that she can take on the world but also actually has more resources to do so. Research has shown, for instance, that in the workplace, highly satisfied employees are more likely to take on new responsibilities and bigger challenges.[24]

Positive emotions expand the repertoire of human capabilities: the physical (for example, the ability to outmaneuver a predator), intellectual (for example, a detailed cognitive map for finding one's way), and social (such as the ability to form lasting and supportive relationships).[25] In the long term, the value of positive emotions is to provide durable resources that a person can draw on over a lifetime. The evolutionary difference between negative and positive emotions is similar to win-lose as opposed to win-win encounters.[26]

Recognizing the Positive Principle

There are four significant ways in which we as Appreciative Coaches can apply the Positive Principle with our clients to help them be at their best:

1. Affirming and appreciating our clients

2. Nurturing clients' expression of positive emotion

3. Helping clients enhance their reflected best-self portrait

4. Building virtuous cycles

Affirming and Appreciating Our Clients

We know from our own rich experience with AI in organizations that people need lots of positive feeling and positive social bonding to make lasting affirmative changes in their lives. A person's positive core expands as it is affirmed and appreciated by others. This positive emotion not only affects how a person is today but also influences his ability to change and move towards a new future.

Moving clients from negative to positive perspectives of themselves and their situations is absolutely fundamental to the Positive Principle. The affirmative capacity to tune into the most positive aspects of another human being is a remarkable human gift; we are partners in the construction of reality.[27] The Positive Principle entails accepting at a fundamental level that human beings are essentially modifiable, are open to new development, and are products of the human imagination and mind—that is, "we are made and imagined in the eyes of one another."[28]

When we affirm and appreciate our clients, we pull them away from self-oriented preoccupation, enlarge their focus on the potential good in the world, increase their feeling of bonding with others, and move them to act in more altruistic and prosocial ways.[29] We guide them, if they are willing, to a "learned helpfulness" (in contrast to the well-documented link between negative affect and learned helplessness).[30] Starting the coaching relationship with a Client Information Form (see Appendix B) and with appreciative questions are two ways we ensure an affirmative and appreciative process with our clients.

Nurturing Clients' Expression of Positive Emotions

Positive thinking and positive emotions build on themselves. When we speak about the benefits of positive emotion, we do not mean to imply that we ask our clients to put on a happy face when they are in stressful situations. A service representative who continually faces disgruntled customers and who must remain pleasant and optimistic throughout these interactions can experience stress, burnout, and job dissatisfaction.[31] In Appreciative Coaching, we do not ask clients to fake an emotion. Rather, we work with them to find their wellspring of positive emotions and motivation. If a client comes to us in a discouraged state, we can consider how we might help him take the first steps in creating a positive reinforcing cycle. We can do this by tapping into our own positive source.

As we have discussed, emotions are contagious, so our affect can have an impact on our clients, whether we are engaged with them in person or on the phone. Our emotions can rub off on them; just by being with us they may feel better (or worse). If clients come to us discouraged or frustrated, we can support them by simply holding on to a positive frame for them. We can help them not to go deeper into their negative emotion, but to take our nonverbal invitation to move to a more positive cycle. Conversely, we need to be careful not to join with them in negative language and affect.

As coaches, we need to be aware of what may stimulate positive emotion in our clients and to help them identify experiences or memories that trigger pleasant feelings. They can thus learn how to amplify those experiences and memories and identify other situations where a more positive outlook is possible. Furthermore, our clients can then broaden their knowledge, build their skills, and increase their personal resources for moving forward. We create opportunities for our clients to experience these feelings in the coaching session itself. A playful, engaging, exploratory, and generous coaching experience provides our clients with profound opportunities to learn and grow that will last long after we are gone from their everyday lives.

Helping Clients Enhance Their Reflected Best-Self Portrait

A *reflected best-self* (RBS) portrait is a life-long construction each person composes by reflecting on extraordinary moments or situations in her life. These are moments when the individual feels that her "best-self was brought to light, affirmed by others, and put into practice in the world."[32] Over time the person collects these experiences into a portrait or image of who she is when at her personal best. At times this portrait may be composed gradually and without much self-awareness or attention. At other times, there may be clear triggers in the environment that change her portrait, such as feedback from the individual's work organization, work relationships, or goals to be accomplished.

Regardless of how the individual comes to extraordinary moments or situations, the portrait serves as a beacon or personal touchstone of who the person is and a guide for who she can become.[33] The RBS portrait encompasses a person's current strengths (competencies, talents, values, and personality attributes) that she can actively use to create value, actualize her potential, and fulfill her sense of purpose.

The RBS portrait is considered a *reflection* because the individual identifies the personal qualities and characteristics that make up his portrait through experiences with others. The portrait is based on the person's perceptions of how others, such as family members, friends, acquaintances, and coworkers, view him. As you might expect, the best-self concept is often based on a patchwork quilt of imperfect and incomplete reflections from others; therefore, people form individual perceptions rather than an absolute "truth" about themselves. The word *best* refers to their strengths, contributions, and enduring talents that they bring to a situation. People compose their RBS portraits through interpretations of positive experiences and interactions in the social world—in other words, through positive relationships with others.

A person revises her RBS portrait in response to "jolts" or trigger events in the environment that act as catalysts to changes in her self-perception.[34] Positive changes related to a jolt are most likely to occur within individuals who have the social resources that equip them to respond with a capacity and willingness to see themselves differently. There are three specific resources that play an important role in revising someone's RBS portrait favorably: (1) positive affect—that is, positive emotions like joy, peace, hope, or gratitude; (2) positive relationships with others; and (3) a sense of being one's own agent—that is, able to make things happen through one's own action. These resources are integral to the Appreciative Coaching process.[35]

Also significant for Appreciative Coaching is that jolts can be brought about by challenges or by appreciation, and they can be generated by formal or informal mechanisms. Challenging jolts take a person out of his routines and offer opportunities for action. To respond to jolts, he has to let go of the known, be open to possibilities, seek out novelty, be curious, and be willing to take risks. Appreciative jolts are immediate experiences of attention, valuing, and affirmation that cause the person to change his self-expectations, bring up positive emotion, and move to a more positive self-image—all of which can lead the person to positive action.

Building Virtuous Cycles

The more we can support our clients in finding pride in their strengths and success in new results, the more they can step into a positive cycle and speed up its rotation. The Positive Principle is about guiding our clients to develop *virtuous cycles*—positive self-reinforcing cycles in how they view their own thoughts, emotions, and actions. The concept of virtuous cycles has been around since the 1950s in such disciplines as cybernetics, economics, and management theory. The cycle describes how one good thing leads to another. It's obviously the opposite of the more commonly known *vicious cycle*, in which a bad thing leads to a worse one.

A virtuous cycle involves a situation in which improvement in one area leads to improvement in another area, which then leads to further improvement in the original area, and so on. It involves all the elements of the Positive Principle that we have talked about— how affirmation and appreciation help build a positive core, how positive inquiry leads to positive change, how positive emotions build the capacity and skills to be creative over the long term, and how best-self portraits are built by personal reflection on positive past and present experiences and positive social experiences. Coaches are instrumental in guiding and reminding clients to create and maintain positive self-reinforcing cycles of thought, emotion, and actions.

Susanna's Story

Often, challenging and appreciative jolts are met with a sense of fear, threat, and cynicism instead of with a sense of possibility for seeing oneself in a more positive place. Mary, Debra, Michelle, and Joe, introduced at the beginning of our discussion, all reacted negatively to their jolts. It is not at all unusual for coaches to encounter this with clients. Individuals who tend to focus on the negative, potentially punishing effects of jolts are less likely to revise their RBS portraits.[36]

Those who focus on the positive, potentially rewarding effects of such experiences tend to revise their portraits positively. Our role as coaches is to help clients see the positive effects of their personal and professional jolts. Following is the story of Susanna's eight-month coaching journey to revise her best-self portrait.

Susanna, a successful lawyer in a prestigious firm, was approaching a professional milestone: moving from associate to partner status. It would be one of those challenging jolts that could be a great opportunity if she were able to respond positively.

As the end of the year approached, Susanna was feeling pressured by a number of challenges she felt she could not meet. She was behind in booking her required billable hours. This would soon become public to her colleagues. The shortfall was due in part to her having taken time away from the office to tend her sick mother. But it also reflected her seeming lack of ability to meet some basic work expectations. Although her firm was in the process of shifting its focus away from exclusively valuing billable work and toward a broader appreciation for nonbillable work designed to increase expertise and develop long-term client relationships, billable work was currently still what counted. Susanna and her mentor believed that as one of the few females rising toward partnership in the firm, Susanna might benefit from coaching to help her get back on track.

Susanna was hard working, dedicated, and loyal to the firm, but by the time she turned to a coach for help, she was in a negative self-fulfilling cycle of feeling depressed and discouraged. She was not working efficiently and couldn't make herself produce. One symptom was her inability to focus during the day. Instead of concentrating on the cases requiring research and response (what she most loved to do), Susanna found herself answering e-mail and avoiding the work for which she didn't see a successful outcome. She and her mentor had tried looking at her situation from different angles. He had given her many suggestions for becoming more focused, organized, and productive, but nothing seemed to work.

In outlining a typical week for herself, Susanna began by describing interesting clients and assignments, but quickly fell into talking about the interruptions, distractions, and demands placed on her and other lawyers.

She was bewildered by others' ability to cope with this stress. The harder she tried, the more she seemed to fail and the worse she felt. She was clearly in a negative spiral of overburdening herself, then avoiding production goals due to lack of time, then questioning her abilities, and eventually allowing her overall self-concept to decline.

Susanna's coach realized she needed some immediate relief from the constant negative messages she gave herself and from seeing only her deficits as a person and as a lawyer. In their initial meeting with the coach, Susanna and her mentor responded to the coach's appreciative questions by describing what Susanna loved to do and was good at: she obviously had a quick mind, was able to see issues from many angles, and had a gift for writing thoughtful and articulate opinions. This was work she loved and that was valued by the firm, but she never seemed to have time for it.

Her coach shifted the conversation to the positive emotions and flow that Susanna felt when she was at her best. Susanna immediately cited mornings as her preferred time of the day—sitting with coffee, doing a little work, and then exercising before arriving at the office at eight o'clock. But she seemed able to achieve that only on Mondays. The rest of the week found her getting up later and later and giving up the things she most enjoyed to make it to work by eight.

In reflection, Susanna realized she was trying to get to work by eight because that's what she thought other successful lawyers did, even though her firm allowed associates to set their own schedule. They could even work at home when appropriate. Susanna hadn't taken into account that she had her own natural rhythm and that she was at her best when she followed it. This "Aha" experience quickly led to some positive actions and experimentation with a variable time schedule.

Susanna's coach repeatedly asked her to identify and describe her strengths and abilities, eventually leading her to a more positive self-perception. Another defining moment occurred when Susanna realized that by not giving herself time to use her higher-level, strategic thinking at work, she was actually depriving herself and her firm of legitimate, billable work. Her shift to the positive was complete when she realized that doing what she really loved at work was a win-win for all.

As Appreciative Coaches, we can do a great deal to create and maintain a positive foundation for our clients to work from. For example, we share our own positive emotions with clients, and model positive connections in our coaching conversations. We can also be the initiator of positive and challenging jolts to help them develop their own personal resources.

Appreciative Language

Positive language is clearly fundamental to ensuring that the Positive Principle is woven throughout our coaching relationships. Staying in a positive frame of mind helps ensure that our positive emotions will be contagious and that we can maintain the positive for those clients who come to us momentarily dispirited. Table 3.2 is a sampling of appreciative language we found rooted in the Positive Principle.

Summary

In this chapter, we talked about the interplay of five principles fundamental to the DNA of Appreciative Coaching. We talked in detail about the two core principles, the Constructionist Principle and the Positive Principle, both of which are drawn from the rich experience of AI in organizations.

Appreciative Coaching is designed to create powerful social experiences (through coaching sessions and life experiments) that help individuals discover the best about themselves. The expression of the Constructionist Principle is fundamental to ensuring that clients move toward an appreciative perspective of themselves and their situation, that they move toward appreciative language in speaking about themselves, and that they build a more holistic and balanced view of themselves.

The Positive Principle as applied to Appreciative Coaching involves helping clients generate and express positive emotions; urging clients to create sustainable positive connections to others,

Table 3.2. Examples of Appreciative Language Rooted in the Positive Principle

Client Language	Coach Language
That excites me. That's a good plan.	I like to hear that word—it excites you.
I feel good about . . .	What are the times you feel at your best?
I think that is on the right track.	
That's what I'm trying to practice—to be really conscious of what I'm doing that day.	What gets you to the point of feeling solid about . . .?
	So you're feeling good with what we have so far?
I've been learning to really appreciate what is happening in this moment.	I love how you're already putting form and substance to this.
It sounds good.	I think that's such a great question.
I am lighter with that.	That's very exciting. You're very talented.
I look forward to that.	
I realized how positive . . .	I see something in you today that I have not seen before.
I feel better about myself.	
	Here is where you will shine.

including the coach; providing appreciative and challenging jolts for clients in the form of insights, experimentation, and new practices; and helping clients build a sense of their own potency and potential as creators of their own future.

In the following chapter, we talk about the remaining three principles that complete the DNA of Appreciative Coaching (the Simultaneity, Poetic, and Anticipatory Principles), and the unique understanding they bring to our perception of time and change.

4

The Foundation of
Appreciative Coaching—Part II

The Simultaneity Principle, the Poetic
Principle, and the Anticipatory Principle

*I have an almost complete disregard of precedent, and
a faith in the possibility of something better. It irritates
me to be told how things have always been done. I
defy the tyranny of precedent. I go for anything new
that might improve the past.*

Clara Barton (1821–1912),
American Civil War nurse,
founder of the American National Red Cross

Our aspirations are our possibilities.

Robert Browning (1812–1899),
English poet and critic

*R*ory made his living as a medical secretary, but his heart wasn't in it.
On the side, he taught yoga and did massage, which fed his spirit and
made him happy. He really wanted to have a job doing something he
loved, but he had been raised with the belief that work was job security
and that your real life happened outside of it. However, he nurtured the
hope that his life could have other possibilities.

A day came when he decided to act, to take the risk of starting his
own yoga studio and massage business. About four months away from
opening his new business, Rory found himself, instead of excited, worried about things from the past—thinking about past failures and his dis-

appointments about projects or ideas that hadn't come to fruition, about whether things would be any different with this business.

When he wasn't reminding himself about his past faults, he found himself worrying about the future. A seemingly endless list of "what ifs" kept him awake: What if nobody came to his studio? What if nobody liked him? What if no one was interested? He felt discouragement from the past and doubt and uncertainty about the future. What was happening to his hopes and dreams?

When he realized what he was doing to himself, Rory had an idea. To pull himself out of the mental and emotional vicious cycle of being stuck in the past and lost in the future, he chose to focus on the present. He took his watch and painted the word NOW in large letters on the clock face. He wore the watch every day as the construction on his building was coming to a close. He relates how that really helped him accept the present moment as a gift to be taken advantage of—isn't that why they call it the present? He began to see the "now" as the only time he had for really achieving change—whether in his mind, business, or body.

After three successful years in business, Rory reflects back on how the NOW watch became his anchor. He couldn't change the past; it was gone. He couldn't change the future; it wasn't here yet. But he could change his present.

Time and Possibilities

As coaches, we are in the business of possibilities, of helping clients like Rory bring forth their potential and open up their range of choices about their lives. Rory came to realize that each present moment was pregnant with possibility and choices for him. Sometimes the weight of the past and the uncertainty of the future prevent our clients from moving forward or seeing themselves in a different light. As coaches, we can do for our clients what Rory did for himself—help them focus on the present.

The three Appreciative Coaching principles presented in this chapter focus on the unfolding of possibilities. The Simultaneity

Principle recognizes that inquiry and change happen at the same time; that is, the seeds of change—how clients think, talk about, discover, and imagine the future—are sown in the first questions we ask. The Poetic Principle invites clients to view themselves, not as problems to be solved, but as an open book of possibilities—as a story that they continually rewrite and that incorporates the learnings of the past, present, and future. The Anticipatory Principle relates to clients' creating a clear positive image of the future for themselves, one that expresses their desires and possibilities; it is this future image that will guide clients' current actions and behavior.

In Chapter Two we talked about how the traditional worldview of an objective, predictable, and controllable universe has given way to a new paradigm of change that encompasses complexity, chaos, subjectivity, interconnectedness, and the use of language to create social reality (social constructionism). Inherent in this new paradigm is an expanded view of time that incorporates multiple causality, discontinuity, and wholeness. We see this expanded or holistic conception of time as underlying all five principles, but particularly the Simultaneity, Poetic, and Anticipatory Principles.

In our coaching research, as we began applying and tracking the Simultaneity, Poetic, and Anticipatory Principles and the Constructionist and Positive Principles (presented in Chapter Three), we noticed that all the principles shared a common perception of time and change. We found this orientation, with its focus on the present and the future, to be liberating, in contrast to traditional beliefs about time and change that emphasized the primacy of the past.[1] The social sciences adopted this traditional notion of linear time from the physical sciences, which viewed the world as static, fixed, and built on unchanging universal laws.

How coaches think about time can have a profound influence on their guidance of personal and professional change processes. Our clients' perspective on time and the way they think about the past, present, and future exert influence on their everyday behavior. Clinical psychologists agree that the temporal orientation or perspective of each individual is central to his well-being and his ability to cope with life's difficulties (and opportunities).[2] Is there hope for the future? Can the past be overcome? What actions and decisions can be made now?

In the next sections, we compare the traditional (Newtonian) view of time to a more holistic and expansive view. As we present each of the three principles, we discuss the pivotal role an expanded view of time can play in helping clients effect lasting change. Our clients can realize their possibilities only by reconsidering how they view the past and by moving forward in time. How we help them do that can create coaching breakthroughs.[3]

The Traditional View of Time

Western philosophers and scientists have studied time for well over twenty-five hundred years and are still confounded by its mystery.[4] Humans first framed their understanding of time as cyclical and marked it by recurring events, such as the daily change from light to darkness; the succession of seasons, planting, and harvesting; and the biological changes of human birth, aging, and death. Later a linear view of time replaced the cyclical. Western theologians played a major role in this shift: with the spread of Christianity came the beliefs that the world has a beginning and end and that important events, such as Christ's birth, are unique and unrepeatable.

In the 1600s, physicist and mathematician Sir Isaac Newton articulated his concept of Absolute Time, portraying it as an unchanging physical reality, independent of human consciousness or choice.[5] His conception altered society's view of time by reducing it to the narrow interpretation of a mental construct. Newton's Absolute Time no longer included individuals' lived experience of time, including intuition and sudden leaps of insight or change. It quickly became the primary, even the exclusive, way time was viewed and understood in Western society.[6] As Newtonian time became synonymous with clock time, the earlier, more subjective experiences of time received much less attention from physical and social scientists. Although this linear view has been helpful to the management of our complex lives, the restriction to a single perspective of time has also contributed significantly to our stress. In the last thirty years, however, with the rise of the new paradigm introduced in Chapter Two, the study of time has broadened to include a more holistic interpretation.[7] For example, in the new sciences, the mind and environment are understood as simultaneous parts of a greater gestalt or life-space.[8]

In the next sections, we will contrast the characteristics of linear time with a holistic perspective of time, including how each of these perspectives affect our perceptions of change. If you are not interested in the theoretical distinctions between these two frameworks, we suggest moving forward to the sections describing the principles themselves, beginning with the Simultaneity Principle.

Characteristics of Newtonian Time

The legacy of Newtonian time has had a significant impact on modern psychological explanations and theories of change, especially in that external, linear time was considered essential to explaining such notions as causality, change, process, and behavior.[9] In the following list, we look at the five characteristics of Newtonian time: linearity, objectivity, continuity, universality, and reductivity, and we consider how each of these characteristics affects the way people view their world and themselves.

1. *Linearity.* Time proceeds along a fixed line from past through present to future. The present is only one brief moment on this line. The past holds supremacy (as the point from which all succeeding events take their cause) and explains the present.

2. *Objectivity.* Time exists independent of human consciousness. As all events occur across time, humans store the past as an objective entity that cannot be changed.

3. *Continuity*. Time is continuous, gradual, and sequential. Inconsistent or discontinuous events (an inspiration, a transformation) are not accepted as valid explanations for change.

4. *Universality*. The nature of time is universal and independent of any particular situation. Its rules apply across cultures.

5. *Reductivity*. Each moment in time is discrete and thereby reducible; nothing exists as a whole at any one point in time. Subject and object are separate—one must precede the other.[10] A later event cannot affect an earlier event.

A Holistic View of Time

The acceptance of Newtonian time in clinical and social psychology resulted in a predominantly deterministic, externally oriented view of change in individuals and groups. Thus the locus of control was almost exclusively outside the individual, and the individual was largely considered the sum total of his past. Although historically most psychological explanations incorporated the characteristics of Newtonian time without question, some psychological theorists and natural philosophers (such as Heidegger, Piaget, May, Husserl, Whitrow, James, and McGrath and Kelly) did not.[11] These individuals wished to account for the lived experience of time in everyday life, which could not be explained by the objective, externally defined framework of Newtonian science.

In the following list, we have selected those themes that provide the greatest understanding of the expanded or holistic view of time that we believe underlies Appreciative Coaching, and we review them using the same five characteristics of time discussed earlier.[12]

1. *Linearity*. Past, present, and future are an integrated whole. The past is only one possible influencer of action and change. The present and future are equally valid influencers.

2. *Objectivity*. Time is a shared perception of reality that can differ depending on culture, society, and family. Individuals

experience time differently depending on circumstances. Because it is subject to reinterpretation, the past is as dynamic as the present and future.

3. *Continuity.* Change may be discontinuous—that is, abrupt, sudden, and qualitative in nature. The past does not determine the present or the future.

4. *Universality.* A shared meaning of time varies from culture to culture and from context to context.

5. *Reductivity.* The individual parts of a process (for example, past, present, and future) can be fully understood only by seeing them as a whole. Later events lend meaning to earlier events.[13] Subject (the individual) and object (the environment) are intertwined as one; they are not separated in time.

Holistic Assumptions About Time

The positive methods we've reviewed in earlier chapters are implicitly supported by this expanded view of time as a framework for growth and change. Inherent in this holistic view of time is the simultaneous interplay of past, present and future, placing equal emphasis on the influence of the past, the power of the present, and the potential of the future to lead to individual change. Following is a list of holistic assumptions about time that we feel are inherent in an appreciative approach to change. You will find that these assumptions underlie the three principles addressed in this chapter.

- Past, present, and future co-occur as an integrated whole, and each part is influenced by the other parts.

- Both the present and the future can influence change in people.

- Being agents of their own actions and attitudes is necessary for people to have self-responsibility and human dignity.

- People can reconstruct the meanings of their past.

- People can change in ways that are inconsistent with their pasts.

- People are best understood in relation to their present contexts.

- People have access to multiple experiences of time.

The Simultaneity Principle

> Much of our view of the world is formed from our ideas of order.
>
> David Whyte, English poet and author,
> The Heart Aroused

The Simultaneity Principle underscores the power of the present in effecting personal change. Inquiry and change are not really separate moments in time, but they are simultaneous.[14] A premise of this principle is that the very questions we ask of ourselves and of our clients laser attention in a certain direction, intended or not, and sow the seeds of change. The questions we ask as practitioners of change set the stage for what our clients find.[15] What they discover in that process (whether it be about the past, present, or future) becomes the linguistic material for the stories out of which they can conceive, talk about, and construct their future. Asking the right question can lead to an "Aha" experience for a client; it can cause a sudden shift in perspective, like a twist of the kaleidoscope, so that a new view appears, freeing the client from the tyranny of his past or his fear of the future.

The holistic assumptions underlying the Simultaneity Principle incorporate a nonlinear view of time, in which simultaneous events can influence one another even if these events are separated across space. For example, studies in quantum physics demonstrate that electrons can simply disappear from one quadrant and reappear in another instantaneously. Holistic social scientists believe that as the present changes, so do the meanings of the past and future, and as the past and future change, so do the meanings of the present—simultaneously.[16] This view is exemplified by Jung's notion of synchronicity, whereby two or more events seem to happen coincidentally, but in fact have a meaningful relationship to the person experiencing them.[17]

Theorists working within the new paradigm assert that there is constant interaction between the person and environment with no temporal sequencing—that is, the environment influences the person and the person influences the environment in the same moment.[18] Neither one precedes the other in time; therefore, one can have an immediate impact on the other. This is the dynamic between inquiry and change that is embodied in the Simultaneity Principle. We inquire into the lives of our clients from the present, and by doing so we give them access to their past and to the potential for their future.

We, and our clients, may not be sure where a powerful inquiry may lead, but as coaches, we can help our clients access their full gestalt of experiences, dreams, and hopes, all of which exist in the present. Within our clients, the past, present, and future exist as a web of relationships unknown to us. The mystery is in what change our inquiry can trigger.

Recognizing the Simultaneity Principle

As Appreciative Coaches, we can follow inquiry strategies to help our clients move in the direction they wish to go:

- Begin the coaching relationship with appreciative questions, which are powerful in reminding clients of their strengths and successes.

- Realize the power of questions and be thoughtful in forming those questions.

- Ask questions that prompt new thinking and answers (whether about the present, past, or future).

- Ask questions that help clients reframe their past from their perspective in the present.

In short, change occurs the moment we ask our clients a question. Our inquiries spark and direct attention. The energy and effort resulting from that attention can determine the feelings and actions of our clients as they move forward.[19]

Patty's Story

Patty was in her mid-sixties and raising one of her grandchildren, a sophomore in high school. As part of her desire to be coached, she wanted help in starting a new career or reentering an earlier career in real estate. Despite the doubts of her grown children, she had dreams of running her own part-time business once she updated her knowledge and became focused on what she wanted to do in real estate.

Initially her coach spent time asking Patty questions about her dreams and probing more deeply into what her business would be and what skills she would need. Patty and her coach began by building her confidence in her ability to learn and relearn on a college level. Through thoughtful inquiry and some confidence building, Patty formed a picture of what she wanted to create (a business as a mortgage loan officer) and some steps to move forward, but she felt she had no foundation to work from. Although she had worked successfully as a Realtor and loan officer in a bank in the past, those experiences seemed to belong to someone else. She was having trouble remembering or tapping into the skills and successes she already had in this area. She landed a job as a junior mortgage loan officer working on securing loans by phone, but was intimidated by all the young people she worked with, who seemed to be quicker thinkers and better on the computer. Patty seemed to forget all the life and career experience she had accumulated over the years in building relationships with people. It was as if her strengths and past experiences had been erased from her consciousness.

Her coach wanted to help Patty reconnect with her past successes as a way of overcoming her present fear. By repeatedly reminding Patty of her past career in this area and pointedly asking her questions about what she did then that had made her successful, the coach reassured Patty that she could live her dream. Every session, her coach inquired about Patty's existing skills and abilities and asked for stories of when she worked successfully as a Realtor and loan officer. Even though she was often on the verge of giving up, Patty would try to respond to the inquiries. Over time Patty started to become more positive about her capabilities for her current job.

After numerous sessions of inquiry focused on helping Patty see the relationship between her past successes, her current abilities, and her future dream, her coach received a surprise e-mail from Patty: "Thanks for the reminder of my past successes. It worked! I have one closed loan, a very happy satisfied older lady. I have one more in process to close next week and I signed a lady yesterday and have three more possible loans. The relating to people is the key . . . the rest you can learn. You were right—thank you, thank you, thank you."

Inquiry creates change, as Patty's story clearly shows. By responding to questions, Patty gradually reconnected with the parts of herself that knew she had the abilities and knowledge to be successful in this new venture. Guiding Patty to remember that she had already done the work was more helpful than merely assuring her that she could do it. The power was within Patty to realize her dream.

We have found that the more inquiry the coach conducts, the more easily the client responds in ways that are meaningful for his growth. The client learns to trust the simultaneous connection between inquiry and what it will trigger. In established coaching relationships, sometimes coaches have only to begin forming a question, and clients are immediately responding from a place of most significance for them. And in some cases, clients begin the inquiry leading to a change entirely on their own.

Appreciative Language

Powerful questions are significant to most coaching methodologies.[20] As indicated by the Simultaneity Principle, Appreciative

Table 4.1. Comparison of Appreciative Questions to Problem-Solving Questions

Problem-Solving Questions	Appreciative Questions
Tell me what the problem is.	What gives you energy?
Tell me what's wrong.	What do you most value about yourself?
What are you worried about?	What do you want more of?
What do you need help with?	What worked well for you before?
What's bothering you?	What's working well now?
What's working? What isn't working?	What first attracted you to . . .?
	What did you do to contribute?
What are you going to do about . . .?	What does it look like when you . . .?
	How will you know?
How are you going to fix this?	What's been your experience with that?
Tell me what you want to do next.	
What do you think caused this to happen?	How do you want to keep moving forward for yourself?
What's your solution?	What are you doing each day that's living your dream?
What's your plan?	

Coaching considers inquiry to be the very avenue to change and thus fundamental to its theoretical foundation. What may be considered unique to Appreciative Coaching is the primary focus on appreciative questions. Table 4.1 is a sampling of these kinds of questions, as opposed to problem-solving questions.

The Poetic Principle

> *The line is an evolving path that actually changes according to the first steps we ourselves take to begin the journey.*
>
> *David Whyte, English poet and author,*
> The Heart Aroused

Elizabeth had been focusing, planning, and hoping for an early retirement from her organization so that she could start a new business. She had been working with her coach for two years on gradually building her dream business and designing what it would look like. She had already begun aspects of it during time off from her job. She had made the move from full-time to part-time work, taking much effort to reduce her workload so she would have energy and time for what she loved to do. It wasn't financially smart to leave her organization, but if she were offered early retirement, she could afford to realize her dream. Over several months, she had heard mostly positive messages that her company was planning on offering this option to its managers. She was going to be ready when the time came, and she was excited.

On the next call with her coach, Elizabeth was down. She had gotten the news from a very reliable source that her company would not offer the early retirement option this year. In fact, she wasn't sure if they would offer it in the next few years. It was a major disappointment, and her coach wondered how Elizabeth was going to react. Elizabeth and her coach started talking about how it felt and what it meant in terms of options for her moving forward. Suddenly Elizabeth's tone shifted. It was as if she took a deep breath, set her shoulders, and made an internal decision to take control. Her coach listened in fascination as Elizabeth began to outline what she was going to do.

If she wasn't offered early retirement, she would start incorporating what she loved to do in her current job. She realized that it was her choice to stay in the job for financial reasons. Maybe there would be some real benefit in practicing what she loved to do in the organization where she was already well known for her excellent work. She started identifying steps she needed to take, which her coach quickly wrote down. Elizabeth had practically coached herself! She had reinterpreted her situation and created new options. She sought and found new possibilities. Although she wasn't sure of the outcome, she reworked her situation positively to move herself forward. This is what the Poetic Principle is all about.

The appreciative approach recognizes the power of stories and metaphors to capture human potential. The client's remembering and sharing stories of when he is at his best can be a powerful incentive when he is struggling to achieve positive change in a challenging life or work situation. Recognizing the range of choices a person has in any given situation and the freedom he has to view his situation from multiple points of view is at the core of this principle. In AI, practitioners talk about the Poetic Principle from the perspective of endless interpretive possibilities and use of the metaphor of an open book—that is, they see the organization not as a machine (with fixed, working parts) but, in essence, as a story that is constantly being coauthored by drawing from the past, present, and future of those in the organization. Like a poem, the organization can be "read" and interpreted in multiple ways.[21]

We find that this principle applies equally to Appreciative Coaching. In fact, it is exceptionally powerful in freeing clients from limited ways of viewing themselves, their environment, and their range of possibilities. A holistic view of time informs this principle: as humans we are not limited to a linear progression through life that emphasizes the influence of the past over the present and future. We are also not limited to predictive cause-and-effect explanations that restrict our ability to reinterpret or rewrite our own stories. But this knowledge is hard for some clients (and coaches) to accept. The pervasiveness of Newtonian time causes us to hold a narrow understanding of the relationship of linear time to cause and effect. For example, we believe that concepts like cause and effect happen only in a linear sequence.[22] Our definitions of causation have been so constrained that we see alternative definitions as unscientific or mystical (for example, Jung's concept of synchronicity) and dismiss them without any formal investigation.[23]

When people adopt a holistic time perspective, they can see that the past, present, and future co-occur, that the past is dynamic (changeable), and that their memories change as they reinterpret their life story to bring them greater meaning in their present and future. With this perspective, people also know that change can be discontinuous: it can be abrupt, life changing, and instantaneous.[24] Linear time does not allow for such phenomena.

In coaching, the Poetic Principle reminds us that our clients live in systems of mutual interaction and that their future cannot be predicted with certainty but instead is made up of probabilities that flow from the decisions they make. Elizabeth was faced with a dramatic change in her expectations. She could have chosen any number of reactions, ranging from an automatic negative response based on past experiences to a proactive decision attuned to the future. She chose the latter. We would like to think that her familiarity with an appreciative approach to coaching influenced her decision. What we know for sure is that through the coach's application of the Poetic Principle, clients are given the choice to reinterpret or reframe their direction and the way they view and understand themselves. Thus, they are no longer limited by the traditional view of time and change that dictated that they were the sum total of their past.

Recognizing the Poetic Principle

We've found two significant ways to apply the Poetic Principle when coaching:

1. Give clients the freedom and permission to see themselves in a holistic way.
2. Help clients connect with their own "inner flow."

The first way is to give clients the freedom and permission to see themselves in a holistic way—one not limited by past actions, current stresses, or future fears. If we as coaches truly believe that individuals have the capability to reinterpret their life story, we will convey that trust and invitation to our clients. Second, the Poetic Principle can help clients connect with their own "inner flow." This is possible only if we help free our clients from the narrow view of linear time that disallows a full range of human expression and autonomy.

Wendy's Story

In Wendy's eighth session with her coach, she experienced a "poetic" moment. She had sent her coach some writing before the session to capture where she felt she was, and during the session she talked repeatedly of finally understanding that feeling of flow in her life. She used such language as, "I think I'm finally getting it . . . that you try things, and if they don't work, you let go of them, clarify your intention, and become open to new possibilities."

Wendy talked about a certain amount of tightness that has been in her body all her life around striving to make an outcome materialize. But she realized that "sometimes you have the intention and it just doesn't work out. Maybe something better is going to happen, or maybe that's not what's intended to be. Sometimes you don't have control." She recognized that there are some things you can push through but that it may not be the best thing for that moment. "It's like, what dream am I living?"

Wendy thought about how, for the past nine years since she went into consulting, she had been really driven and had just kept pushing and pushing. Now she wanted to be open more to the synchronicity of things and move in a more dynamic way. She wanted to keep reminding herself that this moment in time is as important as any moment in the future. She felt as though she had spent much of her life working toward the future, forgetting to be fully present in the moment. "What has been part of my journey for the last five years is really trying to appreciate what's happening in the moment."

Wendy decided she wanted to practice being fully present and clear about her intention for the day and to notice when things flowed well and took care of themselves so that she would not be fighting her own energy. Toward the end of the session, Wendy observed, "It's just been amazing that I now feel like I can see certain aspects of myself that I wouldn't have seen before in a million years."

Wendy could see herself in a different light. As though she had turned a kaleidoscope, she had a new vision and appreciation for herself and how she wanted to live in the present, according to her own inner flow. It's a remarkable experience to witness a client's leap of insight—a discontinuous change that affects the individual holistically.

Appreciative Language

The Poetic Principle is very evident in the language used by both client and coach. As coaches, we are always listening for moments of creativity and discovery on the part of the client. The client's language reflects his openness to positive interpretations of the situations in his life, whether they happened in the past, are taking place now in the present, or might occur in the future. Any language around feeling more of a flow to his life and less of the need to control or hang on to particular outcomes is a sign that the client is opening himself to a creative view of his life rather than hanging on to a deterministic picture of his choices that is more past oriented. Table 4.2 is a sampling of appreciative language we found rooted in the Poetic Principle.

The Anticipatory Principle

> *Whether you think you can or you think you can't,*
> *you're right.*
>
> > Henry Ford (1863–1947),
> > *founder of Ford Motor Company*

The two major elements operating in the Anticipatory Principle are imagination and the creation of a picture of the future. A person's image of the future is what guides his current actions and behavior; like movie projectors, humans are forever projecting their future expectations ahead of themselves through their language and use of metaphor.[25] Appreciative Coaches are especially attuned to nurturing their clients' positive expectations and encouraging them to anticipate and be proactive about their future.

As coaches, we want to redirect our clients from negative self-fulfilling prophecies ("Why bother? This always happens to me. I try, but

Table 4.2. Examples of Appreciative Language Rooted in the Poetic Principle

Client Language	Coach Language
I think this is the trail I'd like to go down.	Let go of a way of life you've had.
	You sound very congruent.
I am in that flow now.	Imagine all your possibilities.
How different! I can move on.	Where have you been successful?
I am already making the	What does that mean for you?
transition, and it's such	A wonderful blessing.
a breeze.	A connection between . . .
So something is happening.	Exploring what you are capable of.
I can choose; help me to	What a great insight!
understand . . .	Reach that energy that's there.
I could strengthen . . .	I see something in you that I have
I don't have to wait.	not seen before.
I need to let go.	You are more yourself now.
It makes me feel grateful going	What will help you tap into
through these challenges.	your passion?
I'm pretty fortunate.	Now you can move on.
It's kind of like, wow!	So some space is opening now,
There is a trust within me now	with possibilities.
that was not there before.	
Putting form to . . .	
The promise I made to myself . . .	

nothing changes. What choice do I have?") to positive expectations of what is to come ("I trust I can do this. I know what I want. I've got my support. I'm sowing the seeds. My intent is clear. It will come."). It is our job as coaches to hold clients' positive expectations, especially through the times of doubt and mistrust, because we understand what a powerful creative force those images and expectations are in influencing what is to come. The Anticipatory Principle in Appreciative Coaching is based on two observations: the power of image and of positive thinking, and a holistic or expanded view of time.

The Power of Image and of Positive Thinking

In formulating the principles of AI, Cooperrider set out to research the relationship between positive imagery and positive action, paying specific attention to identifying where positive images of an unknown and neutral future came from in the first place.[26] His inquiry took him across a wide range of social sciences, including studies of positive imagery from athletics, research into relationships between optimism and health, placebo studies in medicine, studies of the Pygmalion effect in the classroom, and cognitive studies of internal dialogue. He found that the power of imagery has been documented throughout the ages and across the world—from Aristotle to Einstein, from individuals to nations. One need only think of Buddha, Christ, Gandhi, Mother Teresa, and Martin Luther King Jr. to conjure up lasting images of what they stood for. In essence, it is a human trait to hold self-images and to create images of our potential in groups and as individuals. The mind has an astounding capacity for shaping reality by linking positive image with positive action.

As we've seen in earlier chapters, extensive research affirms the power of positive thinking.[27] Past studies of the power of self-fulfilling prophecies show how individuals tend to conform to others' expectations of them, commonly known as the Pygmalion effect.[28] Recent research demonstrates that people's expectations about their own lives go beyond the topic of achievement to include "visceral, emotional qualities"; that is, "our expectancies not only affect how we see reality but also affect the reality itself."[29] Individuals with a strongly positive belief about themselves take on more serious challenges, relinquish difficult tasks less easily, and see themselves as capable and successful, even when they experience failure. This positive belief in the self is built by parents, teachers, mentors, and life experiences.[30]

Expanded View of Time

At the core of the Anticipatory Principle is the notion of the simultaneity of past, present, and future—that is, an expanded view of human time that challenges the traditional psychological assumption that the past is a powerful determinant of the future. A person's image of the future is like a movie on a screen—so if she believes she is bound by the past (by negative self-fulfilling prophecies), then she tends to project a future that re-creates the negatives of the present. People are usually unaware that they project these negatives, and they wonder why the future does not bring them something positive. If instead they believe that they can envision and create a different future for themselves and they do that by being proactive in the present and creating positive expectations (or positive self-fulfilling prophecies), they are functioning with a holistic perspective of time. They are using the present to identify what is best about the past, and they carry that forward into the future they desire.

If a person is bound by the traditional linear view of time, he has little choice about the past: it takes precedence, and he carries its full weight into the future as though it were a very heavy box. In the holistic view, a person can choose what he'd like to carry forward from the past because the past is always constructed from the vantage point of the present. The past has dynamic meaning as it relates to and influences the present and future—it is not static and fixed. As coaches, we help our clients focus on the best of what was, what is, what can be, and what will be—a rich interrelationship "bridging memory's treasures with high visions of the future."[31]

Recognizing the Anticipatory Principle

The most effective way of ensuring that we are working with the Anticipatory Principle in our coaching is to solicit and listen for phrases our clients use to paint images of, and express longings for, their desired future. Our job is to engage our clients in drawing forth and shaping their dreams of the future and to remind them of the crucial link between future images and current actions. We focus on the guideposts listed here as we work with our clients in creating positive expectations of the future:

- Positive images create positive futures.

- Vision is "fateful"; we create our future in the present.

- We create vision before we make decisions.

- What we believe is what we will conceive.

- A grand vision starts with small steps.

- We have more confidence and feel more comfortable journeying to the future (the unknown) carrying what is best about the past (the known).

Terry's Story

Terry was a potential client. The coach was invited to meet with him about business coaching and strategic planning, of which Terry had little knowledge. A successful business owner, he ran an employment service, which brought in over $2.5 million in revenue. You would never know this from Terry's perception of his business. In the course of hearing about his company, the coach began to notice the language that Terry was using. Every other sentence had the word "problem" in it, and many times when he made positive statements, he would follow it with "but" and then add something negative. As they talked about how Terry could grow his business, the coach found they went round and round: every opportunity turned into a problem with the "but" clause. It seemed he could not imagine a different future for his business.

Finally the coach asked if she could make an observation, and Terry gave his approval. She pointed out that he seemed to be stuck. He thought a moment and then agreed with her. Although he wanted to take some proactive action, he found he just wasn't doing it. Then she pointed out the negative, problem-oriented language he was using. Again, he thought a moment, agreed, and added that his wife had pointed that out to him as well. Then he revealed that he came from a poor family, had never had big expectations for himself, and was always worried that he could be back in a position of having no money. The coach pointed out how successful he was in his business, and he again agreed; he just didn't usually think of himself in that way.

The coach explained how the past did not dictate the present and future—in Terry's case, this was obviously true. She stated that the past was not immovable (like a very heavy box), but changed and evolved depending on where a person was in the present. Terry seemed to be listening intently and quietly nodded. The coach used the metaphor of Terry's having the power to pick up a kaleidoscope and with a slight turn of his hand create a new image of his business from a more positive perspective, one in which he could enjoy his position as president of a challenging yet successful company.

Then Terry had an "Aha" moment. He realized he was stuck because the company was now in a stable financial position after working itself out of a tough time four years ago. He recognized that he didn't want to make any major changes for fear of returning to an unstable position. Terry and the coach agreed that his focus for this year would be to add just one big new client and to maintain his current clients. This was an image he was comfortable with. He looked up at the coach and said he felt better already. As she was driving back to her office, the coach reflected on how vulnerable Terry had been with her to reveal his fears from the past and how real it was that we all have the power to choose how we want to view the present and future.

Appreciative Language

Inquiry is a powerful tool we can use to serve our clients as they anticipate their future. Questions that help them paint positive images of the future are most helpful, especially as many people we work with may be reluctant to believe they can actually achieve a long-buried or long-nurtured dream. If you remember, Patty was raising her grandson and had the dream of reentering the workforce as a mortgage loan officer, something she hadn't done in almost twenty years. Her dream was like a small ember that needed attention to help spark it into life. Asking her questions about successes in her past that she could carry forward into the (unknown) future gradually built up her level of confidence and comfort to actually move in that direction. As we discussed with regard to the Simultaneity Principle, inquiry and change happen at the same time.

In addition to inquiry, another coaching tool involves using our clients' images and stories about the future to inspire them to do something. Facts or figures seldom prompt people to take action, let alone risks; positive images and stories are what provide the road map.[32] Kathy, the financial representative who had the dream of building up her business and becoming financially stable, decided she needed to create a theme for the year: "leadership and growth within my business and myself." Once she identified that image for herself, she began taking action to make it happen; she became proactive with her business associates and began inquiring into leadership opportunities. She anticipated a positive image of her future and then began to make decisions to act toward that future.

As with all the principles underlying Appreciative Coaching, the Anticipatory Principle evokes positive, appreciative language that helps move clients in the direction they most want to go. Table 4.3 is a sampling of appreciative language that illustrates the Anticipatory Principle.

Summary

In this chapter, we discussed linear time as a powerful concept that permeates how people view themselves and their ability to change. It is a concept so fundamental to people's way of thinking that they are often unaware that they are guided by a view of time that considers the past to be a determinant of their present and future. We also presented an alternative, holistic view of time that better accounts for the many ways we experience it. This multiplicity exists in all human life and change. Someone may experience time as a flow state in which he is entirely unaware of its passage or as the source of transformation during which leaps of insight cause him to reinterpret his past. The holistic view of time affirms that people

Table 4.3. Examples of Language Rooted in the Anticipatory Principle

Client Language	Coach Language
I now look forward to . . .	How does that feel as you
That excites me—it's a good plan.	anticipate . . .?
What am I practicing to get me there?	What about that excites you?
	What images do you have of . . .?
I'm being real clear about my intention for the day.	Who are your role models for . . .?
There will come a day when I feel right about doing this and then I'll do it.	What are some ways you'd like to challenge yourself with . . .?
	What could you imagine yourself doing?
If I described my wish list, I could be pointed in the right direction.	How do you want to keep moving forward for yourself so that you keep doing the kinds of things that you'd like to around this?
I'd like to imagine myself . . .	
I'd like to come up with . . .	So would that be something of interest for you in the future?
	What's a small step that could take you in the direction of doing more of what you want?
	That's an excellent step to get you where you want to go.
	What would you like that to look like?

create their future through their current choices and attention. All of us are agents of our own actions and change.

We also presented three Appreciative Coaching principles: the Simultaneity Principle, the Poetic Principle, and the Anticipatory Principle. Each of these is grounded in a holistic view of time. In our discussion of the Simultaneity Principle, we demonstrated how inquiry and change happen simultaneously. By asking powerful, positive questions, coaches enable clients' ability to direct attention in ways that can increase clients' belief in their capacity to take fruit-ful action in moving forward. In our discussion of the Poetic Princi-ple, we showed how a holistic view of time can allow clients to reinterpret their past so that new possibilities can open up for their future. In discussing the Anticipatory Principle, we illustrated how our clients' imagination not only creates an image of the future but also anticipates their actions and thoughts toward that desired future.

With the next chapter, we begin to present the methodology of Appreciative Coaching. Chapter Five discusses how to begin an Appreciative Coaching relationship with a client. Chapters Six through Nine explain the Appreciative Coaching stages: Discov-ery, Dream, Design, and Destiny, respectively.

5

The Appreciative Coaching Process
Getting Started

*Genuine beginnings begin within us, even when they
are brought to our attention by external opportunities.*
William Bridges, American theorist and writer on
managing change in organizations

To become a practitioner of Appreciative Coaching is to accept
a core belief about our clients and how they change: individuals are mysteries to be appreciated. We do not see our clients as problems to be solved or as deficient in some way. Our job is not to fix them. Our job is to partner with them in a positive, generative approach in which they are agents of their own change. They are not passive vessels but decision makers with the potential (and inalienable right) to master their own lives through their choices and preferences.[1] At times, our clients will have problems to resolve, but clients themselves are not problems. This is a profound distinction for us that we have grown to respect as a result of our appreciative research and experiences. We discovered early in our research process that beliefs in the deficiencies of humans (especially when it comes to our own frailties) are deep seated.

Acknowledging the core belief that individuals are mysteries to be appreciated is the first step in getting started as an Appreciative Coach. We know from experience that it is a challenge to hold that belief when working day to day with clients, especially when faced with our own negative feelings of frustration, self-doubt, sadness, anger, or fear. Such negative responses are as contagious as positive emotions. Yet we feel it is our responsibility as Appreciative Coaches to hold on to this belief for our clients. To help us follow this core belief, we use the Appreciative Coaching principles as our foundation and the Appreciative Coaching stages as an action process to follow. In Chapters Six through Nine we outline each of the four Appreciative Coaching stages: Discovery, Dream, Design, and Destiny.

In this chapter, we begin with a brief review of our Appreciative Coaching model. We then set the stage by sharing some learnings from our research and experience with appreciative language that are fundamental to how we create the coaching relationship. Next, we present a way to start the coaching conversation from an appreciative perspective and provide a template for forming the coach-client relationship. We then present a format for how you might conduct the initial coaching sessions. We end the chapter by suggesting ways to work with clients who present inspiring opportunities.

The Appreciative Coaching Model

Our model is based on the four stages of Appreciative Inquiry: Discovery, Dream, Design, and Destiny.[2] At the center is the naming of the topic for the coaching relationship, which in Appreciative Coaching is stated in positive or at least neutral language (to avoid slipping into a problem-solving perspective). Although in theory the stages are sequential, actual practice shows them to be very dynamic and iterative in the overall coaching relationship. In our illustration of the Appreciative Coaching model (Figure 5.1), there are arrows leading from one stage to another, beginning with Discovery and leading clockwise to Destiny. But to show the interrelatedness of the stages, there are also arrows internal to the model to illustrate that any stage may lead back to a previous one, such as Dream back to Discovery or Design back to Dream or Discovery.

Figure 5.1. The Appreciative Coaching Model

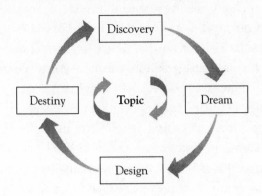

We discuss each stage in detail in the following chapters and provide examples from actual coaching conversations. These will illustrate the focus of each stage and how they are interrelated in leading clients through an appreciative process. The Appreciative Coaching process is not time bound, in that coaches and clients determine the length of time for any given coaching engagement.

Setting the Stage

In conducting our coaching research, we identified distinctive language that we believe may be unique to an appreciative perspective. These distinctions arose from working with our clients, who revealed differences in the way they described various topics, pictures of success, goals, and dreams. Although most coaching approaches begin with a client's goal for the process, we begin Appreciative Coaching with identifying a client's topic.[3]

Clarifying the Topic for Coaching

We use the term *topic* as a neutral framing for what clients perceive (at the beginning of the coaching relationship) as the subject of the coaching process. The word *topic* is neutral; it implies neither good nor bad, weighty nor light, hard nor easy. We prefer to use "topic" instead of "goal" so that we can lead clients to present their issues, concerns, or challenges in a neutral or positive manner as something they would like more of in their lives. For example, we would want to reframe a client's initial desire to "correct deficiencies in the area of staff management" into the more positive topic of "what I need to do more of to become an effective manager" or into the neutral topic of "getting better at staff management."

Starting with "correcting deficiencies in staff management" begins with a negative premise—the individual has shortcomings to overcome. This is not an uncommon goal for managers after receiving the results of a 360° assessment. Performance appraisals usually stress challenges or deficiencies,[4] and development plans lay out steps to overcome them. Appreciative Coaching begins by reframing problems into a neutral or positive topic ("getting better at staff management"), which begins the coaching relationship with a very different kind of inquiry (and therefore catalyst for change) for both coach and client (Simultaneity Principle). We might begin by asking,

- What are the times when you are at your best as a manager?

- Talk about some peak experiences you've had as a manager.

- Who do you admire for their skills and abilities in managing staff?

- What are one or two things you'd like to do more of as an effective manager?

The topic focuses the coaching process, particularly in the Discovery Stage, when there is a great deal of exploration about the past and present skills, talents, and successes of the client that relate to the topic. While exploring the various features of a client's life, the coaching conversation can appear to be drifting. The topic sets a clear boundary and provides a foundation for exploration of its positive aspects as it relates to the client. The coach can hold on to the topic as an anchor and can relate conversations back to it by identifying common threads and learning.

Forming a Picture of Success

After clarifying and stating the topic for the coaching engagement, we work with our clients to help them communicate a picture of success for their coaching topic. Although this may seem to be an obvious step, we have found that some clients are better at describing what they no longer desire rather than what they would like in its stead. Considering the Constructionist Principle—people amplify what they attend to—it is critical to spend time in formulating some picture of a successful engagement. This step may be especially important for corporate clients who need to document the benefits of coaching.

We help clients be as descriptive as possible, but their picture of success may not include measurable items at this point. Often the very things that make for success can be observed or felt but cannot be quantified. We focus on three areas we would like clients to think about in forming a picture of their success: What are they doing? What are they feeling? How are they regarded by others?

Continuing with our example of "getting better at staff management," we might ask our client the following questions to help her form a picture of her success in this area:

- When you are faced with a challenging management situation, what does taking decisive action look like?

- What are you doing as an effective manager?

- What does it feel like when you are comfortable and confident in handling management situations?

- What do you need so as to feel on top of your game as a manager?

- How does your staff feel being part of a well-managed department?

- What do employees most appreciate about your management style?

- What would being "well regarded by others" mean to you?

- What support do you give other managers who come to you for advice on handling their management situations?

Forming a picture of success enhances and builds on the topic identified and framed by coach and client. Spending some time on a picture of success is an especially effective antidote to clients' feelings of being weighed down by a problem-solving approach or a primarily negative perspective of their situation. Clients often feel stuck when using negative language, and we've found that moving them to a place of positive, generative language and images helps break the negative cycle and starts building some positive emotional capital for their journey forward.

Setting Goals in Appreciative Coaching

After we have clarified the *topic* and *picture of success* with the client, we turn to his goals. In contrast to topic, goals identify specific ends for coaching and reflect language that is more commonly associated with planning or problem-solving approaches, such as achieving measurable results or improving oneself (either in terms of overcoming deficits or making use of one's potential). Goals identified early in the coaching process serve to keep the purpose of coaching in sharp focus and set the expectations for a successful conclusion, but they can also be confining if they do not provide room for exploring a client's successful experiences and talents and if they do not take into consideration the full texture of a person's life.

Timing is a key factor in the naming of goals. Beginning with goals instead of a picture of success may impede the appreciative process if coach and client do not give time and attention to building a positive context for the goals. After first building a positive frame for the client, the coach can then lead her to express some goals (for example, build opportunities with staff for two-way communication, develop an employee recognition and reward process with staff input, get training in effective management and leadership skills). In Appreciative Coaching, however, we find that moving directly from topic to goals doesn't always provide our clients with a large enough context for them to tap into their true interests and passions. We usually like to spend some time in the Dream Stage before helping clients articulate specific goals.

Expressing a Dream

As opposed to goals, a dream is a picture of a desired future that the client is willing to work toward. It provides a bigger canvas or larger context for the client's intentions and interests to manifest in various ways. As the second stage in Appreciative Coaching, Dream focuses on the client's imagining a larger frame as a sort of container to hold his specific goals or needs. He can articulate a number of goals to fulfill a dream.

Going back to the topic of "becoming better at staff management," we imagine that our client has responded with positive memories, experiences, and desires about what she would like to do to become a better manager. At this point, it can be quite fruitful to ask the client some questions appropriate to the Dream Stage, like these:

- How do you envision yourself as a great manager?

- How would effective staff management enable you to do that?

- What successes do you see yourself celebrating as a manager?

- What vision do you have for yourself in the next few years?

- What legacy would you like to leave behind?

Without fail, the answers to these kinds of questions come from deep inside the client. The insights help her recognize her yearnings and excitement about life. Tapping into that energy and passion can help the client place the topic of "getting better at staff management" into a more meaningful context. Having done so, the client then finds it easier to set goals around a positive or neutral topic so that they are based on the deep desires of a future dream.

Another Wendy Story

The language around topic, picture of success, goal, and dream is now distinct for us as we work with clients from the appreciative perspective. This story is about Wendy, the consultant whom you first met in Chapter Four. She helped us see and experience the significance of how tapping into a person's dream creates the context for setting goals. Wendy participated in coaching before we clarified the distinctions among topic, picture of success, goal, and dream. Her story exemplifies how those distinctions affect our coaching process and how we too learn from our clients.

Wendy came to coaching knowing that she wanted to improve marketing for her business. This became her topic for coaching. Her coach, following a protocol she had learned prior to practicing Appreciative Coaching, looked to develop goals for the coaching engagement and asked Wendy how she would know her marketing had improved. Wendy replied that she'd have more clients. And, to make things very clear and quantifiable, she was prompted to identify that this meant six new ones.

As sole proprietor of a small coaching and training firm specializing in diversity, Wendy revealed during her first encounter with her coach that she saw marketing as something she was not very good at. As much as she disliked it, however, she saw it as a necessary part of her business, and she wanted to become comfortable doing it. During the Discovery Stage, Wendy identified activities she excelled at and enjoyed, and as she did, her coach asked questions to relate these to her topic of becoming better at marketing. Wendy talked about her love of music and storytelling and how she effectively used storytelling as a learning tool in her diversity workshops and in her coaching. She was a gifted storyteller. Drawing on these successes, her coach asked Wendy to consider how storytelling could be used in marketing.

Reflecting on this potential link (an entirely new and unanticipated direction for her), Wendy thought about how her stories had morals or teaching points, which she connected to her clients' concerns. She realized that if she were more mindful about the ending or moral of a story, she could use it in marketing as a means to engage someone in conversation—much as she did in a workshop. Listening to the stories of potential clients, she might be able to provide a learning experience that would hold some lesson for them and perhaps interest them in continuing a relationship with her. This just might engage prospects to ask her about the type of work she did. Then she would be marketing!

All this exploration in the Discovery Stage resulted in a variety of examples of how her many abilities and interests could be used in marketing, but Wendy felt they were disjointed. She had no larger context to frame these possibilities for her. She decided that she wanted to be led through a guided meditation to help her see her future picture, her dream. She asked a colleague with this expertise to guide her. The meditation resulted in a dream of marketing that brought together and integrated the skills, successes, and talents she discovered during the Discovery Stage. She created a picture of what storytelling, music, and art in marketing would look like for her, and she saw the types of groups she could interact with and how.

As she filled out the picture of her dream, she saw herself engage others by bringing out their life stories, using images and art in her marketing materials, and employing song as a way to focus and soothe. Marketing in this way felt easier for her because it was using her skills and natural talents. Once Wendy created her dream, her energy and enthusiasm for marketing changed appreciably. She no longer saw it as something that she needed to make herself do. She shifted from seeing marketing as something unpleasant that had to be done to something that was a natural way of expressing herself that she enjoyed.

Once her dream was clear, she began setting some specific goals to actualize it. She began working with her marketing materials to see how *she could weave in her art and music. Now that she was more comfortable going to networking groups, she thought about what specific marketing actions she could take when she was there, such as using her stories as teaching opportunities.*

Wendy's experience enabled us to see the great potential during the Discovery Stage of helping clients identify their topic for coaching, describe a picture of success, and only later create their dream, followed by developing goals. Having Wendy step back from her initial goal of finding six new clients allowed her to spend some time exploring the topic of marketing as it related to her past successes and current skills and abilities. She was able to tap into positive memories and feelings rather than focus on her weaknesses. In their conversations, both coach and client discovered that for Wendy there was more to improving marketing than just acquiring clients. Becoming comfortable and feeling capable were part of Wendy's picture of success that she had identified initially. Creating a dream gave her the frame for making sense of the many possibilities she had for marketing that was based on her love of stories, song, and art. She developed a comfortable context for herself in marketing her services to others and discovered many avenues to engage them in creating their own dream stories.

Forming the Relationship

Having clarified the distinctions among topic, picture of success, goals, and dream, we are ready to discuss the process of forming the coaching relationship. We use protocols similar to those of other coaching methods, so in this section we highlight only those that may be unique to Appreciative Coaching.

Getting Acquainted

We have worked with clients about whom we knew very little and with clients whom we did not know at all. As experienced coaches know, building trust is a critical element of any good coaching relationship. In fact, the relationship is the key element of success in the helping professions.[5] Entering into a relationship, clients need to know us as much as we need to know them. This process of getting acquainted is important not only as an opportunity for clients to gain confidence in the abilities of their coach, but also because we are in fact beginning the Appreciative Coaching process itself by activating the Constructionist, Anticipatory, and Positive Principles. As coach and client share knowledge of each other, they begin to form a social bond. As the coach shares her knowledge of how other clients have experienced and benefited from coaching, the client may begin to see possibilities for himself. And as the client feels and hears positive expressions, he may begin to pick up hopeful emotions.

Clarifying the Topic

As we stated earlier, we like to see clients begin Appreciative Coaching with a topic instead of a goal. If clients begin by speaking in terms of difficulties, issues, and problems, we help them reframe these into a neutral or positive topic. If clients begin by sharing specific goals and excitement about something they want for themselves, we move toward a reframing of the specific goals into a positive, slightly broader topic. We simply start where our clients are and gently help them see their possibilities for moving in the direction they want their lives to go.

When clarifying the topic, we use the five principles as guides in directing the conversation. Each principle suggests a course of action or demeanor. First, our questions guide clients toward their own answers (Simultaneity Principle). If we ask for further information about a problem that the client has presented, she will go deeper into the details and emotions of the situation. If instead we ask for what she hopes the situation will be like at the end of coaching, we may get answers that spring from a creative perspective. Second, by focusing on what the client wants, we help her form a more positive phrasing of what is possible (Anticipatory Principle). Third, this may help the client see that with our support, she is able to change what she is facing (Constructionist Principle). Fourth, relating to the client in these ways and helping her see her abilities creates positive affect or feeling that what she wants is indeed possible (Positive Principle). Finally, as the client begins to create a vision for her future, she may see herself quite differently in that future (Poetic Principle).

Tools for Getting Acquainted with Your Client

We have developed an appreciative Client Information Form (CIF) (see Appendix B) as a general tool to help us get to know our clients more quickly and to provide them with an immediate experience of an appreciative approach. We give the CIF to the client after an initial meeting or phone call and before we begin the coaching engagement. We often customize the form depending on our client's circumstances. The CIF collects contact information and consists of questions organized into different sections. The questions are constructed to help the client focus on positive traits, abilities, accomplishments, and desires. The form explores five major areas:

- *Your History* asks the client to reflect on how accomplishments in his past may relate to his present and future.

- *Your Life* asks the client to contemplate and identify supports he can draw on.

- *Your Self Today* asks about how he lives his life.

- *Your Potential* explores what the client would like to achieve in the future.

- *Making It Happen* asks about the client's preferred approaches to making change happen.

The information that is collected provides background and context to help us understand the client's responses to the four core questions (discussed later) when we are ready to ask them. The information in the CIF also assists in exploring the client's topic. The CIF can be revised to suit a particular coaching purpose and style; however, we recommend that revisions maintain the focus on the Appreciative Coaching principles.

Other tools that can help acquaint us with the client may come from the client herself or from our own toolkits. We ask the client for any results she may have from formal feedback tools, such as a 360° instrument or personality test. These are very useful in getting to know clients, but we caution that many of these instruments are based on a deficit approach to assessment rather than a strengths-based one,[6] which would be more compatible with an appreciative approach. If we must use a deficit-based assessment instrument, we work with the information to find a positive fit with the framework of Appreciative Coaching. Restating the deficit as a broader topic in neutral or positive language is usually possible. We also ask clients for results of any workplace feedback instruments received within the prior twelve-month period. We have found that these can give us a broader perspective on what the coaching topic might entail. Most experienced coaches already have a collection of preferred tools. We suggest looking at them with an appreciative filter using the five Appreciative Coaching principles.

The Initial Coaching Sessions

Our first few coaching sessions can be much more prescribed than the succeeding ones. In these, we review the CIF questionnaire, ask the core appreciative questions, and begin to explore the pathways of constructive futures.

The First Session

The purpose of the first session is threefold: to begin setting the appreciative context through the coach's use of appreciative language and inquiry, to review the information from the CIF with the client, and to begin the Discovery Stage by asking the client the four core appreciative questions that identify and clarify the client's neutral or positive topic for the coaching contract.

After we receive the completed CIF and any other information we may have about the client, we plan our first session by reviewing our data from an appreciative perspective. Information about achievements and past successes provides the most obvious food for thought. If the client has written about problems or disappointments, we think of ways to help him recast his situation in more positive terms.

The first session then begins with an exploration of the CIF. We ask questions that we believe will give us greater insight into our client from her answers or in the way she explains or expands on her answers. An important learning for us has been to listen for and inquire directly into how our client felt in answering the CIF questions. The expectation would be that positive questions would elicit positive responses, but that is not always the case. Sometimes clients react to the questions by feeling intimidated or inadequate. Maybe they have never stopped to contemplate their thoughts on a particular subject.

Bill, owner of a successful computer software company, reacted to the questions on the CIF by commenting on how hard some of the questions were to answer; they caused him to think a lot and reflect on the fact that he wanted to spend more time with his family. Carolyn, a successful Realtor, also found the questions very thought-provoking, causing her to be reflective about herself and her life. She said she found herself thinking about how much she really wanted to reveal to her coach, because she did not want to disappoint her. Ultimately she decided to take the opportunity to understand some things about herself. And as we touched on in Chapter Three, some clients are hesitant to claim or recognize their best talents and abilities. Debra, in responding to a request to describe her three greatest accomplishments to date, replied she had little to write—she hadn't saved anyone's life or anything!

After reviewing the CIF, we often devote the rest of the first session to asking the client the four core appreciative questions:

1. What gives life to you now?
2. Describe a high point or peak experience in your life or work up to now.
3. What do you most value about yourself, your relationships, and the nature of your work?
4. What one or two things do you want more of in your life?

From the coach's perspective, the responses to these questions accomplish two major objectives. First, they give the client the opportunity to remember, reflect on, and ponder not only what is important in his life but also what is or has been positive in his life. The exchange begins creating positive feeling or affect for the client—as though he were depositing money in a savings account that he can draw on later. Second, as we have emphasized, inquiry and change happen simultaneously. By beginning with positive, life-enhancing questions, we immediately start moving the client away from problem solving and toward creative, solution-based outcomes in which he is the agent of his own change.

What Gives Life to You Now?

We learn from responses to the first question some of the things our client really enjoys or values. Answers may range from people and places to activities and intellectual pursuits. We find it fascinating to learn how differently people approach and experience life. Understanding the source of a client's energy and interest gives us an idea of the kinds of experiments we can craft later that we can link back to that source.

*Describe a High Point or Peak Experience in Your
Life or Work Up to Now*

Answers to the second question reveal how our client evaluates her achievements, relationships, and environment. Knowing this, we are able to find ways to help our client replicate aspects of her peak experiences in her current situation. We can probe into how our client felt, what skills she used, the type of people she surrounded herself with, and the quality of relationships or interactions she enjoyed in her experiences. As coaches, we refer to these past experiences as examples of success when the client faces challenging situations in the present.

What Do You Most Value About Yourself, Your Relationships, and the Nature of Your Work?

The third question asks the client to identify or recall the best parts of himself and the world around him. By focusing on what he most values about himself, his work, and his relationships, he begins creating a positive context to frame the challenges, issues, or topics he brought to the coaching relationship. Concerns look different when the client views them from a position of feeling capable, respected, and validated. With a continued focus on the positive, the client is usually feeling more empowered by now than at the beginning of the session.

What One or Two Things Do You Want More of in Your Life?

The fourth question asks the client to identify things she aspires to or longs for in her life. Her answer begins to shape a picture of what a possible future may look like. Clients' responses often involve some exploration and probing on the part of the coach. We've found that clients are able without fail to answer this question. In some cases, what emerges is different from their initial topic or intent; in most cases, it brings out a broader perspective on their topic. This underscores that our clients' aims, desires, and needs are open to revision as clients and coach become clearer about the client's possible future.

A few moments may be reserved at the end of the first session to define the four stages of Appreciative Coaching. Whether the coach does so depends in part on the interest or learning style of the client. The coach might point out that in the first session, the coach and client are defining the topic that will be carried through all of the subsequent Appreciative Coaching stages. They are entering the first stage, Discovery, through the core questions, and this process of inquiry continues until both coach and client feel satisfied that they have arrived at a deep understanding of the topic. They have accounted for successes, abilities, resources, and desires related to the topic. As other coaches do, regardless of approach, we give the client a Coaching Prep Form (see Appendix C) and ask him to fill it out and return it before the next coaching call. We follow this process throughout the coaching relationship.

When the coaching session is concluded, we take a few moments to consider and note what we heard from our client and where we think we are in the Appreciative Coaching process.

The Second Session

The purpose of the second session is twofold: to continue in the Discovery Stage to build on our client's positive self-regard in relation to her topic, and to further refine the topic and the client's description of success. We continue getting better acquainted and deepen our understanding of the topic and picture of success by asking the client another set of questions delineated in the Pathways of Constructive Futures model shown in Figure 5.2.[7] This model is especially helpful if our client is having difficulty stating her topic in a positive manner.

Let's return to the topic of "correcting deficiencies in staff management" to demonstrate how to use the pathways model. The coach and client can begin at one of three different points. Using the Hypothetical Frame, the coach might ask, "If your future could be any way you wanted it to be, how would you state the topic of correcting deficiencies in staff management in a positive way for yourself?" Or, working with the Inclusions Frame, the coach might say, "Describe a time when you felt you were at your best in managing your staff." Using Acknowledgments or Gratitudes, the coach

Figure 5.2. Pathways of Constructive Futures

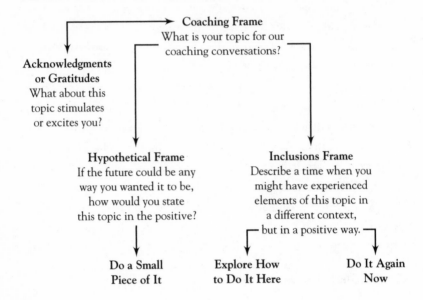

might ask, "What about getting better at staff management stimulates or excites you?" Coaches can also inquire into all three points to really help the client think broadly about her topic. Using these frames, coaches can help clients take beginning action steps.

Sometimes our clients are not able to view their topic in a positive light even after doing the Pathways of Constructive Futures activity. When this occurs, we find it helpful to use a powerful tool from SFBT: the miracle question,[8] described in Chapter Two. The following is a variation of the question: "Suppose that one night, while you are asleep, there is a miracle and the concern that you have is gone. However, because you are asleep, you don't know that the miracle has already happened. When you wake up in the morning, what will be different that will tell you that the miracle has taken place? What else?"[9]

By the end of the second session, coach and client have usually agreed on the focus for the coaching relationship and have identified some of the client's past successes and current capabilities in this area, as well as discussed some idea of what it will look like for the client when he succeeds with his topic. From this point forward, the coaching relationship can vary significantly in how it continues through the Discovery Stage and passes through the remaining three Appreciative Coaching stages—Dream, Design, and Destiny. Some coaching relationships may move quickly through the remaining stages; others may take considerable time alternating between the Discovery and Dream stages as clients work to reframe challenging views of their capabilities or current situation. In all our coaching sessions, we try to be mindful of the language we and our clients are using. We always seek to build our clients' capacity to use positive language by modeling it ourselves.

Clients Who Present Inspiring Opportunities

In our research, we were fortunate enough to encounter another key learning—that clients can present us with great opportunities to learn and grow. We encountered just such a situation during the second phase of our coaching research. After recognizing that one of our clients showed remarkably different responses to core questions than the others, we discovered something that to us was profound—yet so obvious: the client's frame of reference sets the tone and pace of coaching, as Laura's story exemplifies.

Laura, a single mother who had raised two children, was a successful operations director of a small computer company. She supervised eleven other women who did computer problem solving. As part of our coaching research, we taped and transcribed all nine of Laura's coaching sessions and then compared them with the transcripts of the other two research clients. Laura's process and language looked different: her transcripts didn't seem to sound as "appreciative" as the other two did.

Laura's coach began to feel defensive—was her competency as an Appreciative Coach in question? Did she think she was doing Appreciative Coaching but really wasn't? What was wrong? She was sure she had followed the appreciative protocol with Laura, but indeed something looked different. Something had happened that didn't fit with research expectations.

Our discussions revealed an obvious variable. Laura was her own person bringing her unique tone, pace, and experiences to the coaching relationship in three major areas:

1. Her level of past experience and facility with self-analysis and self-discovery

2. Her facility with language to describe and understand herself

3. Her level of positive outlook in terms of herself

The Client's Level of Past Experience and Facility with Self-Analysis and Self-Discovery

Clients bring with them a wide range of past experience and facility in their ability to self-analyze and in their interest in discovering what makes them tick. Some clients have engaged in a lifetime of efforts as adults to better understand themselves—maybe they've already been in therapy, attended leadership training, or enrolled in professional workshops on management or supervision. Other clients may come with little interest, motivation, past encouragement, or opportunity to delve very deeply into themselves. There is a continuum of experience and facility with self-analysis and self-discovery, and each individual is unique. Some individuals are constantly self-analyzing; others are just busy living their lives.

Laura seemed to have had less experience in the areas of self-analysis and self-discovery than the other two clients. She did not indicate whether she had had previous exposure to training, therapy, or other one-on-one adult relationships in which individuals are able to talk about themselves. She noted that she had no formal management or supervisory training. In contrast, the other two clients both described years of self-discovery activity. They'd been involved in or actually led training or leadership classes, coaching, or therapy of some kind. They each appeared to have brought with them a wealth of past experience and success in this area. They were at the far end of the continuum. It was a point of contrast with Laura.

The Client's Facility with Language to Describe and Understand Herself

The second area in which clients can vary is in their facility with language to describe and understand themselves. Here was another area in which Laura seemed to have less experience compared to the other clients. In looking over the transcripts, we found examples of language Laura used when referring to herself: "I could not come up with five adjectives to describe myself when I'm at my best. Because I'm not that way. I'm not a bragger"; "It's very, very difficult for me to analyze myself. . . . Makes me extremely uncomfortable."

In contrast, the other two clients used such language as, "What I value most about myself is that I'm authentic with who I present myself to be" and "I'm an extremely feeling person. I can pick up on people's auras." There were distinct differences in language between these two and Laura.

The Client's Level of Positive Outlook in Terms of Herself

The third area we identified is the level of positive regard or affect clients bring to the coaching relationship. Some clients come with the experience, encouragement, and permission to speak positively about themselves and their growth. Others may not have been raised or educated to look at themselves in that way. Each client is unique.

Again, there was a contrast in this area between Laura and the other two clients. When asked questions about herself and moving into the future, Laura gave the following responses:

- Answering a question about what legacy she wants to leave: "It made me feel inadequate. Like . . . what could I possibly leave behind that would be of any value?"

- Responding to her coach's comment that she has an open mind: "I'm trying to—yeah, it's very difficult with my personality, but . . ."

- Thinking about meeting a soul mate and how wonderful that would be: "Oh yeah, but you know, that'll never happen."

The other clients used very different language in describing themselves:

- "I enjoy my own company; I've never had a problem doing things on my own."

- "You're as much at the mercy of the situation as you allow yourself to be."

- "I was blessed to have those experiences, even the traumatic ones, because getting to my core so quickly . . . forced me . . . to look at reality."

- "I was really clear that that's where I was supposed to be going."

- "In my mind now I have much more of an idea about what my needs are, and so at least I have control over the decisions now."

Although Laura seemed to bring a different level of experience and facility in these three areas, she was not a negative person. She was highly successful, and she enjoyed her life. What we learned from Laura was very inspiring: each client has the inalienable right to be exactly who he or she is in the coaching relationship and to receive no judgment on the part of the coach (*Why can't he talk about his accomplishments? Shouldn't she be more positive?*). Our clients are molded by their past and current experiences, dreams, abilities, and facility with language and change. They set the tone and pace of the coaching relationship.

At first we had assumed that the higher the level of experience in these three areas we've discussed, the deeper and more quickly clients would resonate with an approach like Appreciative Coaching, whose main focus is on positive self-discovery. Yet when Laura completed her final evaluation of her coaching relationship, she rated the experience very high. Even though her coach was not always sure whether Laura was enjoying the process, Laura clearly thought differently and found great value in it. As coaches, we sometimes bring our own "template" or preconception of how a satisfied, positive client looks and acts.

Summary

Our intent with this chapter was to help you get started with coaching from an appreciative perspective. This perspective involves accepting a core belief that individuals are mysteries to be appreciated.

We presented our Appreciative Coaching model, which incorporates the four Appreciative Coaching stages: Discovery, Dream, Design, and Destiny. In this area, a key learning for us was that our language and process with clients should clearly distinguish among the client's topic, picture of success, goal, and dream. We like to begin our Appreciative Coaching relationships with a topic, rather than a specific goal; this topic is articulated in positive or at least neutral language. The client then moves to describing a picture of success. We have found that helping clients move from Discovery into Dream before they begin identifying specific goals gives them a broader context for tapping into the energy and passion they need to realize their desires.

The Appreciative Coaching process begins in the first session: the coach and client review the client's CIF and the coach asks the four core appreciative questions inherent in the Discovery Stage. In the second coaching session, the coach helps the client further refine the topic by asking her questions from the Pathways of Constructive Futures model and, if necessary, the miracle question.

We concluded the chapter with another key learning: that our client's frame of reference is what sets the tone and pace of coaching. Clients are unique and will vary in three major areas:

1. The client's level of past experience and facility with self-analysis and self-discovery

2. The client's facility with language to describe and understand himself

3. The client's level of positive outlook in terms of herself

We best serve our clients if we release preconceived notions of how they will look or respond.

The next four chapters outline each of the four stages of Appreciative Coaching, beginning with Discovery. In each chapter we offer stories, applications, and tools to bring the stages alive.

6

Discovery Stage
Reflecting and Celebrating

*The real voyage of discovery consists not in seeking
new landscapes but in having new eyes.*

Marcel Proust (1871–1922),
French novelist

*No pessimist ever discovered the secret of the stars,
or sailed an uncharted land, or opened a new door-
way for the human spirit.*

Helen Keller (1880–1968),
American blind and deaf educator

Discovery is the first stage of Appreciative Coaching and sets the tone for the process. It is about truly appreciating what gives life to our clients. The purpose of the Discovery Stage is to help clients focus on an appreciative view of themselves and of the topic or situation they bring to the coaching relationship. It is a wondrous responsibility to embark on a journey of discovery with clients. The process may begin with a desire to achieve something very specific, or it may start with a longing to lead a more joyful, ful-filling life. Whatever the focus of the discovery process, it always leads our clients in directions that initially can be exciting, but also a little nerve wracking, as they encounter new ways of seeing and thinking about themselves.

In the Discovery Stage, we support our clients in achieving a positive perspective about their lives that will serve as a foundation for their chosen future. We encourage them to reflect on, celebrate, and make use of their strengths, successes, abilities, and desires and to connect these discoveries to their hopes and dreams for the future. We use appreciative questions to bring out the best in our clients and to provide opportunities for them to see themselves and their situations with new eyes. We enhance their positive core by teasing out stories that illustrate their unique strengths and skills, and we help bring their future possibilities to life.

The Coach's Focus in the Discovery Stage

As Appreciative Coaches, we focus on the following four ideas in this first stage (as shown in Figure 6.1) to bring out the best in our client:

1. Establishing a positive connection between coach and client
2. Leading the client to a more empowering perspective
3. Affirming a sense of the possible
4. Cultivating and supporting the client's belief in a positive future

We begin by asking our clients to reflect more expansively on what they would like to achieve. Sometimes the coach and client spend one session in reflection, celebration, and making connections, and sometimes they have multiple celebratory conversations. It is the quality of the exchange that makes the difference, not the quantity. For those clients who already have the ability to view themselves and their possibilities in a positive light, Discovery is a time to help them celebrate who they are, to look back on what they have accomplished, and to support them in moving forward.

For those clients whose level of positive self-regard is low, Discovery is the time to create a more positive self-image. Some clients

Figure 6.1. Discovery

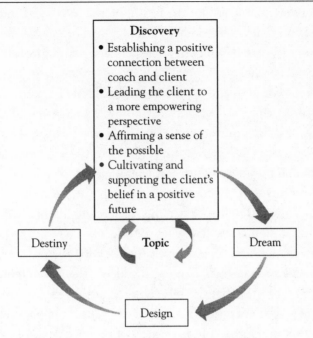

come to us focused primarily on what is not working in their personal or business lives. This may be due to habit or conditioning. Perhaps these clients have a stronger critical inner voice. Unfortunately, not all of us are blessed with a view that our life glass is half full. Sustaining a positive focus may be a new experience for them. Our focus in the Discovery Stage is to move such clients to an appreciative view of themselves and their situation, which can result in the emergence of a more positive, nurturing view of themselves and their future.

Establishing a Positive Connection Between Coach and Client

The coaching profession widely accepts the importance of establishing a positive connection between coach and client. We know from our experience with the positive methods discussed in Chapter Two and from the studies mentioned in Chapter Three that positive emotions are significant for the facilitation of individual and group change and that people do better in making lasting changes when they are supported with consistent personal affirmation and positive social bonding.

Thus, affirming and appreciating our clients is a key factor for establishing this positive connection in Appreciative Coaching. Also paramount is nurturing the development and expression of our clients' positive emotions. As we've seen, positive emotions are contagious, and they play a critical role in undoing the effects of negative emotions in transforming how people think and act.[1] Our positive emotions influence our clients' desire to interact during the coaching session and shape what they decide to speak about.[2] Our encouragement and support open the door for clients to examine new, more creative and life-enhancing ideas. Clients can more readily interpret unfamiliar or ambiguous situations as positive when they are feeling energized by positive emotions.[3] Supported by this understanding of the contagiousness of positive emotion, we can mindfully create an environment that invites more open sharing and creativity. This openness encourages our clients to search for the humor in a challenging situation or to reinterpret that situation more optimistically and confidently.

We can "infect" our clients with our optimism and joy through the demonstration of our firm belief that they have many exciting possibilities from which to choose. We know that we help our clients build positive self-reinforcing cycles because they often report feeling better just by interacting with us. This is another way we establish and maintain a positive connection. If clients come to us discouraged, we can support them by consistently holding a positive attitude and belief in their capabilities.

Finally, of fundamental importance to building a positive connection is our role in gently moving clients from problem language to appreciative language. A major theme of this book is the importance of using appreciative language in every stage of the coaching process. We help our clients reframe their problem-solving per-spectives and negative self-talk through our use of more affirming language. We invite clients to adopt an appreciative perspective of themselves, their past experiences, and their future possibilities through our questions, our responses, our reframing, the tone of our voice, and even our body language.

We talked earlier about Susanna, the lawyer who found herself in a negative self-fulfilling cycle. She acknowledged that she was greatly affected by her coach's ability to maintain and convey a positive belief in Susanna's abilities despite her own self-doubts. Her coach worked to establish a positive connection with Susanna by affirming and appreciat-ing her strengths and abilities, by nurturing Susanna's ability to connect and express her own positive emotions, and by gently steering her toward appreciative self-talk. As the coaching relationship progressed, Susanna repeatedly told her coach that the positive affirmations encouraged and reinforced her self-talk that she was indeed capable. As Susanna regained belief in herself, she received feedback from some of her company's part-ners and associates that they found her to be more confident in her inter-actions with them.

As Susanna's story indicates, an encouraging coaching relation-ship is important to clients because individuals are better able to interact with others and their environment when they maintain pos-itive self-regard. They are more creative, more motivated to high per-formance, and more helpful toward others. Susanna's coach was able to help her create a positive reinforcing cycle that served to support and sustain her as she let go of a negative, critical view of herself.

Leading the Client to a More Empowering Perspective

All of us, coaches and clients, have our own beliefs and worldviews. Some beliefs may limit a client's ability to see new possibilities. After all, as individuals we can only know what we know. Although this may at first appear to be circular reasoning, what it means is that we cannot learn something new without some internal or external stimulus, which may be a book with new information, an experience offering a unique opportunity to reconsider an old truth, or simply a need for clarification.[4] Coaches from all traditions offer great value to clients by opening new perspectives and thereby offering unique responses to clients' desire to learn. Appreciative Coaches are catalysts who spark a new interpretation of an event or a rephrasing of a belief that helps their clients positively reinterpret their life events and situations. The Poetic Principle affirms that there are as many interpretations of every facet of an individual's life as there are interpretations of a poem. People choose where to direct their attention; they can focus on memories of creativity or times of pain. We encourage our clients to remember their peak moments or to find alternative understandings of moments that have been difficult.

People have a choice about whether or not to interpret their thoughts, actions, and beliefs in the most life-enhancing way. Sharing an appreciative perspective with our clients can help them create a more holistic and balanced view of themselves. In our own experiences, we have encountered clients who seem to have strong inner critics that lead them to create negatively skewed self-images. If this self-criticism is overwhelming, it allows little room for a countervailing positive self-perception. These clients may have outwardly successful professional lives but perceive themselves to be imposters[5] or live internally under a negative cloud.

Betty was struggling with a tendency toward procrastination. She described herself as "frittering" or "foot dragging" and as having a "high threshold of resistance" to doing what she thought she ought to do. Yet in reality she had held several positions of responsibility for long periods of time, had been an entertainer who honored her commitments, owned her own home, and maintained a web of close friendships. She functioned well in the world.

Betty was listening to a severe inner critic. With her coach's help, Betty realized that she didn't have to be so hard on herself. She wondered aloud what this procrastination would be like if she could see it differently. Her coach suggested that she might view the procrastination as a door-

way rather than as a barrier. She could stand in the door frame and explore the view—on one side she could consider what she saw without action, and on the other she could take the risk of action. Betty loved this metaphor. She now had a different way to look at what she had seen as "her difficulty": "Maybe I don't want to knuckle down yet," she said. "Maybe I need to have compassion for that part of me that's fearful about a new future." Betty started opening to the opportunity of discovering a new image for herself.

The Simultaneity Principle suggests that the coach's inquiries directly affect the changes clients are likely to make. Where we guide our clients' attention will direct the focus for change; that is, our questions to our clients will suggest their path forward. Inquiring into our clients' talents, past and present successes, and unmet desires is a crucial aspect of the Discovery Stage and helps our clients positively expand their view of themselves. We ask them appreciative questions to remind them of their strengths and successes. Our invitations to reconsider past events within new frameworks may cause clients to reinterpret their life events more generously. We help clients create a clear image of the key attributes they want to keep and build on for the future. They might remember capabilities they had forgotten or dismissed. Seeing these skills in a different context, clients may then reevaluate them. These new interpretations can provide energy to take on challenges that previously seemed impossible.

Affirming a Sense of the Possible

Clients hunger for a sense of new possibilities and are at their most vulnerable when they share these with us. Even highly successful clients may harbor secret dreams along with hidden doubts about their capability of achieving a long-held desire. Or they may feel that the culture and expectations of their workplace stymie their attempts to reach these dreams.

Dan, a plant manager, worked in a company where management had no administrative assistants. Managers were expected to do their own administrative work. Dan often found himself caught up in tactical activities, thereby not always getting to the strategic work the company expected of him. He was increasingly frustrated. His coach began asking him questions that prompted new thinking and answers on his part. She challenged his perception that he was trapped by organizational norms. She asked him how he could reframe his responsibilities to make the best use of his time by freeing himself of the company norms. She prompted him to test his assumptions that there would be negative consequences if he hired some administrative support. She helped him move away from using problem language (what he couldn't do) and toward using empowered language (what he needed to do to perform successfully). Dan's coach affirmed a sense of the possible for him in this situation, and he responded by deciding what he wanted and figuring out how to make that happen.

We consider affirming the possible to be an integral part of the Discovery Stage. By stimulating positive emotions in our clients about their successes and talents, we help assure them that they have what they need to realize new possibilities. Our strategy is to help clients first experience positive feelings about their possibilities in the coaching session, which they can then draw on as they explore and experiment between coaching sessions. Together we build on the knowledge that more is possible.

During the Discovery Stage, Debra, who was unemployed and struggling to follow up with prospective employers, was asked by her coach to describe a time when she felt proud of herself. After some hesitation, Debra described a situation at a wedding in which she "told someone off." Surprised by what seemed to be a negative reply, her coach probed for more details of what made her proud in this situation. After thinking, Debra explained that it was a time when she felt she had stood up for a friend. She was proud that she had overcome her usual reticence to speak out. Her coach reacted positively and with appreciation for Debra's learnings from the experience, noting that she had demonstrated strength and integrity by supporting her friend. Debra agreed that it proved she could speak up for herself. It was a positive example from the past of what she was capable of. Debra then drew on those positive feelings from the past to support her in her current job hunt. She generated enough energy from the positive feelings to begin returning phone calls to some of the companies she was interested in. Her coach had helped Debra reconstruct the meaning of her past experience by valuing and affirming a positive self-image for Debra, resulting in her enthusiasm for positive action.

As we have seen, setting up coaching experiences that are exploratory and safe creates an environment where clients can be more open to their possibilities and we can affirm them. By using appreciative language to help Debra reframe her past from the perspective of the present, Debra's coach helped her construct and identify a positive experience from the past that she could add to her RBS portrait. Her coach's appreciative jolt about her learnings from the experience helped Debra see herself in a more positive light.

Cultivating and Supporting the Client's Belief in a Positive Future

As Appreciative Coaches, we want our clients to move toward the future with confidence and comfort by carrying forward what is best about their past. One of the ways we can do that is by listening for the words, phrases, or metaphors they use that resonate with their future desires.

Rita came into coaching with the belief that she needed to find alternative employment. Although she had felt highly valued in her company for a long time, she believed that this was no longer true. Her company was in the midst of rebuilding its reputation after several unprofitable years, and a new CEO came on board who was more critical and less supportive than his predecessor. Because Rita brought in the lion's share of new business, she felt under particular pressure from senior management to produce new clients. With the transition, she felt others were critical of her performance.

Her coach, listening carefully to the words Rita used, realized that she felt underappreciated. She suggested that Rita pay attention to and observe how she was being approached by her boss and others. Soon Rita realized that her boss and peers were anxious about whether they could bring the company back to its former success, and their expression of anxiety was not personal to Rita. Looking around, she began to see a more positive future for herself in the company. She decided she wanted to help with the transition by doing two things: reconnecting with former clients and observing rather than reacting to the pervasive anxiety among senior managers. She also wanted to encourage her peers and support people to maintain their own self-esteem and productivity. Her real desire was to value others (as she liked to be valued) and to work toward something satisfying over the long term, such as helping the company emerge successfully from this transition.

By adjusting her view of what was going on in the company, Rita began affirming positive images of the organization that then helped create a positive future for her there. Her more realistic appraisal of her current work situation (understanding that she didn't need to take things so personally) resulted in a more empowering perspective.

Before clients are able to paint future pictures for themselves, they must believe in the possibility of that future. This is where we coaches come in—forming a supportive coaching relationship, encouraging an affirming perspective, and engendering a belief in the possible. We are able to support our clients in believing that a very positive future is indeed possible. The more strength there is in this belief, the more clients will be able to stretch and create something that goes beyond their current assumptions or level of comfort. This is what lays the foundation for creating an inspiring dream in the next stage.

A Coaching Sequence in the Discovery Stage

Although we realize that every coaching session in Discovery is unique to the client and the coach, we will describe here an inquiry sequence that we commonly use in this stage. The sequence supports the findings of the RBS portrait process we explained in Chapter Three.

As we noted earlier, people revise their RBS portrait when they experience challenging or appreciative "jolts" or trigger events.[6] Appreciative Coaches can play a significant role in helping clients connect with their RBS portrait by asking them to describe their peak or positive experiences and helping them reflect on the significance of these positive experiences in their current (and future) lives. The coach provides appreciative jolts that engender positive emotions for clients and help them realize they are their own agent of change. Clients begin to act as if they can make things happen!

The following four steps outline a sequence for soliciting positive feelings about the client's present and past successes:

1. The coach asks the client to describe a positive experience.
2. The client reflects on the positive aspects of the experience.
3. Client and coach identify similarities across several positive experiences.
4. The client applies learnings to the topic of coaching.

Step One: The Coach Asks the Client to Describe a Positive Experience

The coach begins by asking the client to recall an experience or situation about which he is proud. This peak experience may or may not be related to the coaching topic. While the client is describing the experience, the coach listens and probes for richer description and deeper understanding, especially of the client's actions, thoughts, and feelings. This description forms the foundation for creating a positive context for the coaching topic—inquiring into past or present successes, skills, and strengths.

Carolyn came to coaching with the topic of needing to organize her personal life. One symptom of this need was that she had failed to file her taxes for several years. She was swamped with household paperwork, details, and tax deadlines. Her home office looked like the aftermath of a windstorm. She was overwhelmed by the number of things she had to do, and didn't know where to begin to dig herself out. Her coach asked Carolyn to share a peak successful experience. Carolyn shared that she was the top-performing Realtor in her office. She had worked hard to achieve that distinction. She enjoyed satisfying her clients with good service and expected herself to perform in a completely professional manner with them.

Step Two: The Client Reflects on the Positive Aspects of the Experience

In the second step, the coach asks the client to reflect on or identify what it is about the peak experience or successful situation that brought him enjoyment, pride, and satisfaction.

Carolyn revealed that she saw her higher purpose in her work life as helping clients find their perfect home. This meant meeting clients' needs, making the process as enjoyable as possible, and enabling them to feel happy and satisfied with their decision. With probing from her coach, Carolyn talked about how she was always timely in completing the paperwork and meeting deadlines for closings. She stressed that being timely was especially important to show respect for her clients and to create repeat customers, thereby building her good reputation. She was proud of being the top performer in her office. She also cared deeply about her clients.

Step Three: Client and Coach Identify Similarities Across Several Positive Experiences

The third step occurs after the client has described a few positive experiences; the situations do not have to be related. The idea is for the client to learn how to reflect on similarities and patterns in his positive experiences and for the coach to learn more about how the client approaches situations. Again, the coach plays a key role in enabling the client to identify similarities by supporting him with positive affect, fostering a positive relationship, and affirming his abilities.

Carolyn shared several positive experiences she had had with clients. They were all similar in that she had acted with utmost professionalism and timeliness. She knew how to deal collaboratively with her office staff to get things done. She kept a calendar, had an excellent filing system to support her work, and had figured out ways of reminding herself about due dates to keep herself organized. Carolyn realized she had learned these behaviors over the years in building a successful career. She had excellent business skills, but she had not translated them to address her needs at home. There her natural style—a more organic and spontaneous one—prevailed.

Step Four: The Client Applies Learnings to the Topic of Coaching

During the fourth step, the coach helps the client circle back to the topic of coaching by asking him to consider which similarities from the positive experience(s) he can apply to his topic for coaching. At first nothing may surface; the question may even feel a bit foolish. But it is important to stay with this step and not rush forward too quickly.

Carolyn's coach asked her if she had ever considered treating herself with the same respect that she showed her clients—applying her organizational skills to the tasks and deadlines in her home life. Carolyn had never truly connected that she could use her skills from her business life in her home situation. It was just not her natural style to be detailed and organized. Yet she did that for others. With this "Aha" revelation, Carolyn and her coach began talking about ways that Carolyn could use her business skills at home. The coaching relationship ended with Carolyn completing a year of her taxes and becoming more organized at home. The notion that most stayed with Carolyn from the coaching, however, was that she would treat herself with the same respect she had reserved for her clients.

This four-step process is a mainstay for us in the Discovery Stage. We find that our clients respond positively to the innate logic of focusing on what works and then seeing how those effective experiences can be applied elsewhere. The process gives clients a sense that there is an inner coherence linking their past and present with their future desires.

Coaching Tools in Discovery

An Appreciative Coaching conversation can take many forms and use a number of techniques or tools. Here we share a few we find useful in the Discovery Stage. You can choose those that seem most helpful to each individual client. When you are reviewing your existing toolbox, reevaluate its contents with an appreciative filter and consider how each tool and technique can help further the discovery of positive experiences, traits, abilities, and desires.

Questions

For the coach, inquiry is the fundamental tool of the Discovery Stage. We ask questions to actively surface good news of opportunities, strengths, achievements, visions, and innovations. Although a coach can ask an endless number of questions, in Discovery we tend to focus on inquiries that help clients see their abilities and past successes, prompt them to think about or see situations in new ways, and help them imagine new possibilities. Appreciative questions have the following characteristics:[7]

- They express curiosity, not judgment.

- They are framed positively or are at least neutral.

- They are open rather than closed—that is, they ask what, where, who, and how rather than ask for yes-no responses.

- They are thought starters ("I wonder what . . .").

- They invite multiple answers rather than seek the "right" one.

- We typically ask the four core appreciative questions (discussed in Chapter Five) at the beginning of an

Appreciative Coaching engagement. They are questions that set the tone and begin the coaching process.

Pivoting

Pivoting is the conscious act of turning attention from what the client
does not want to what he wants. Many times clients tell us what
they do not like in a situation or what makes them uncomfortable.
These negative statements can be a preliminary step to discovering
what clients want in place of their discomfort. Implicit in the negative statements is a desire for something better. The coach can ask,
"What you don't want is x, so what do you want instead?" Eliciting a
response may take a little coaxing, as most people find it easier initially
to describe what they don't want rather than what they do want. Identifying the positive counterbalances the feeling of lack or other negative emotions, and empowers clients to see possible alternatives.

The Positive Principle states that a person amplifies what she pays
attention to. This process occurs whether the object of her attention
is positive or negative. Pivoting helps the client turn her attention to
her positive possibilities, to creating her desired object rather than
amplifying what she doesn't want. When a client finds it difficult to
distinguish between what she wants and the absence of what she does
not want, it may be helpful to have her list possible alternatives and
then to check her emotional responses toward each idea to see which
sparks the most positive response. Together coach and client might
create an initial experiment to test the chosen alternative.

Another example of pivoting is asking a client how a "negative"
trait can actually function as a strength. This takes the client's perceived deficit and turns it into a strength.

*Laura was talking to her coach about a personality trait of hers that
she considered to be a deficit. She compared herself to people who could
think very quickly on their feet and always seemed ready to react. In contrast to them, she needed to think before responding. She reported feeling
uncomfortable when she kept people waiting in meetings while she "got
done thinking."*

Her coach explained the difference between extroverts and introverts and how American business culture favored extroverted behavior, especially in meetings. She informed Laura that extroverts often think while they speak, whereas introverts prefer to think first and then respond. As Laura identified herself as an introvert, she was responding in the way that was most natural and beneficial for her. It was hardly a deficit; it was her strength to provide thoughtful answers. Her coach assured Laura that it was perfectly legitimate to give herself permission to operate in the way that was most successful for her. Laura and her coach then spent a few minutes brainstorming positive actions she could take for herself so that she could take time for her responses but not feel embarrassed when she didn't respond in the moment.

Observation

Prior to taking action or attempting an experiment, the client may benefit from an exercise in observation. The purpose of observation is not for him to criticize or judge but to watch himself carefully as he performs something he would normally do automatically. In setting up the observation exercise, we help the client identify what he wants to understand better. The observation could be about what time of the day he finds most productive, what frustrates him in interactions with a particular person, why negative feelings recur, or anything else the client would like to see more clearly. The coach asks him to clarify the situation in which he would like to understand himself better, then asks him to observe the situation to identify feelings and actions over the course of a day, week, or month.

Some clients prefer more structured observation. If so, they may find it helpful to keep a journal in which they record their responses to the following questions (or any other questions coach or client might want to add):

- What do I want to become aware of?

- When and where will I make my observations?

- What is the focus of my attention?

- What am I thinking about the thing I'm observing?

- What am I feeling about the thing I'm observing?

- How am I acting as a result of my observation?

- What good might come of this activity?

Experimentation

Entering a new situation or attempting to do something one has never done before can be frightening. A person can feel as though she is putting herself at risk if she agrees to try something that she believes she does not know how to do or that she believes can have unanticipated negative results. She may not trust her own skills and abilities, or she may believe that circumstances will not support her in doing well. She does not know whether she will be successful or, if she is, how others might view or react to her.

Experimentation is a concept or tool we often use in Appreciative Coaching because it helps clients approach new situations more easily. Experiments are opportunities for our clients to be curious and playful about the often serious changes they would like to make. We ask them to try something new to discover what happens. We use the word *experiment* to convey the notion that no matter what the results may turn out to be, there is no failure on their part. There is neither any value judgment about the quality of their results nor, by inference, any judgment about them. This lack of judgment creates a measure of freedom to try something without fear of failure or embarrassment.

Experiments are usually assignments clients assume between coaching appointments to try something new and outside their comfort zone, but not so far out that they feel unsafe. If an experiment is completely out of their comfort zone, they may not try the new behavior, or they may do it in such a way that negative consequences occur. In the coaching conversation, we help clients set the experiment at their "learning edge," that space where there is a balance of anxiety and anticipation.

Carlo finished graduate school and quit his job in the same month. He was confident that his newly acquired academic credential would enable him to reenter the high-tech field after having spent several years outside the field in a less demanding administrative position. He and his coach explored the strengths he demonstrated in his academic career as well as in his professional positions. It didn't take long for Carlo to discover, however, that his few remaining contacts in high tech weren't going to produce a dream job for him immediately. He began to work with a consulting firm that helped him find names of current contacts and available positions within the high-tech field. Everything moved along smoothly until Carlo came to a place that really pushed his "learning edge."

The consulting firm identified one hundred contacts in his area most likely to have jobs like the one Carlo sought. He sent cover letters and résumés and then faced the task of having to call to make appointments. This was daunting; he sat immobilized by one hundred names. Carlo's coach suggested breaking the names into three groups: the least likely to have a job that Carlo would be interested in, the most likely to have a job, and a possible job list. Then she suggested that Carlo experiment first with the "least likely" list so that he could practice his introduction with contacts who probably wouldn't have a job anyway. With this plan, Carlo began to feel more confident that he could actually overcome his fear and begin making calls. After all, what was the worst that could happen?

In a few cases, clients benefit from a more structured approach to experiments. In those instances, they create and follow their experiment using the discussion points listed here. We talk about the first three areas with them before they begin and the remaining two areas afterward:

- Idea or skill to be tested

- Anticipated results

- Where and how the experiment will be conducted

- Actual results

- Reflections and learnings

A word of caution is in order about use of the word *experiment*. We have found that clients who work as scientists or engineers usually do not have the same lighthearted approach to the word as we intend in Appreciative Coaching. For these clients, experimentation is a serious matter related to scientific study and is only done with careful deliberation and planning. The word *experiment* conjures up hard work, concentrated attention, and success or failure with significant consequences. It is important to be sensitive to clients' reactions to this concept and, if necessary, choose another term (such as *try out, play with, investigate,* or *check out*) to convey the meaning of playfully trying something with no possibility of failure.

Role Models

The subject matter of Discovery can also include role models, those individuals who serve as resources or examples of what our clients would like to achieve. These individuals can serve as character or performance models outside a client's own experience. For example, a client who was recently promoted to an executive position asked her coach to assist her in taking on the new challenges. During their first discussion, the client revealed that she did not have any description of an executive that would help her know what was expected of her. When her coach asked if she knew an executive whom she greatly admired, she immediately responded with a rich description of that person. In her excitement, the client quickly realized that she had not only the description she needed but also a mentoring resource in that person.

Role models are sources of rich information that clients can use to develop their own picture of how they would like to be viewed. This becomes a point of discovery for what clients already have to build on from their own reserves.

Getting the Most out of Discovery

At the beginning of most coaching engagements, both coach and client feel a sense of pressure to get something done, a predisposition to resolve something. This is fundamental to a problem-solving approach and largely understood as a given in the profession of coaching. We agree that helping our clients take action is one of the cornerstones of our profession. However, we make a distinction between action to resolve and action to inform. The Discovery Stage is more about action to inform—that is, encouraging our clients to experiment, to expand their thinking, to recognize their accomplishments, and to build their confidence and store of positive affect to move them forward so that they have the foundation for a big dream. Clients learn in different ways, and we have found in the Discovery Stage that it's effective to match each client's rhythm of learning. Some people contemplate before taking (resolvable) action; others learn by doing. Some may move quickly through this stage; others may want or need to slow down. It's the coach's job to guide clients through this stage so that they move into the Dream Stage with a stronger appreciation and belief in who they are and what they would like to accomplish.

Summary

The Discovery Stage, the first and foundational step of the Appreciative Coaching process, is about helping clients enhance and focus on an appreciative view of themselves and the topic they bring to the coaching relationship. As Appreciative Coaches, we pay attention to four activities in this stage to ensure that we set the stage for bringing out the best in our clients. We begin by establishing a positive connection with them. Affirming and appreciating our clients and nurturing the development and expression of their positive emotions are key to ensuring this positive connection. Our positive emotions play a critical role in influencing clients' desire to be more open, sharing, and creative in the relationship.

Second, although our clients come with their own beliefs and worldviews, we are there to help lead them to a more empowering perspective of themselves and their possibilities. To this end, we help them achieve a more holistic and balanced view of themselves by inquiring into their past successes and connecting those with their current strengths and future potential. Next, we affirm a sense of the possible in their lives by asking questions that prompt new thinking and by helping them reframe their situation using empowered language instead of problem language. We also play a unique role by offering appreciative jolts about positive past experiences that add to our clients' reflected best-self portrait.

Finally, our clients need a strong belief in a positive future in order to venture forward in a confident and successful manner. As Appreciative Coaches, we want our clients to carry forward what is best about their past. They also learn to nurture positive images from the past and present so that they may apply those images to the future. A supportive coaching relationship, an affirming perspective, and a belief in the possible are all essential elements for success in the Discovery Stage.

We presented a typical sequence of four steps that we use during this stage: describing a positive experience, reflecting on the positive aspects of the experience, finding similarities across several different positive experiences, and then applying those learnings to the coaching topic. We also described coaching tools we use in this stage: inquiry, pivoting, observation, experimentation, and role models.

In the next chapter, we present the Dream Stage. There is a natural flow from Discovery into Dream, the stage in which clients dare to express their desired future.

7

Dream Stage
Articulating Potential

I have a dream.
> Dr. Martin Luther King Jr. (1929–1968),
> Nobel laureate, Baptist minister, civil rights activist

A vivid imagination compels the whole body to
obey it.
> Aristotle (384–322 B.C.), Greek philosopher,
> teacher of Alexander the Great

I have a dream." These simple words spoken so eloquently by Dr. Martin Luther King Jr. on the steps of the Lincoln Memorial in Washington, D.C., on August 28, 1963, elicited a profound response from the overflowing audience. With these words he was able to deeply touch the innermost desires of his listeners and help them believe that it was indeed possible to speak of these desires, and even achieve them. His words are no less powerful now when we hear them spoken on newsreel or see them in print.

As coaches, we also find it profound and inspirational to listen to our clients express their longed-for wishes and desires and to watch them come to the belief that it is truly within their power and ability to achieve them. The purpose of the Dream Stage is to support our clients in articulating a meaningful picture of the future—a picture that is of their own choosing. We encourage them to stretch beyond the limits of their comfortable self-image so that they create a vision powerful enough to inspire and direct them to actualize a true dream.

In this chapter, we present the appreciative process of creating a dream or future picture that is grounded in the five Appreciative Coaching principles mentioned in earlier chapters. Although we are not the only coaches who help their clients dream, this stage is an integral and foundational part of a holistic coaching approach that begins first with our clients' discovery and acknowledgment of their successes, abilities, and strengths. Appreciative Coaching brings clients a unique sense of coherence to their lives because the dream is grounded in and extends from their own past and present. They can believe in it and in their ability to make it real. As all coaches know, the path in creating a dream is not always easy, especially for clients who have not had an opportunity to think in this way before. Facing a blank canvas is exciting because the possibilities are open, but it can be daunting if one does not take it a bit at a time. Having the opportunity to discover and accept experiences of being at their best gives our clients a positive edge as they enter the Dream Stage.

Here we begin with our definition of *dream*, one based on a holistic approach to envisioning the future. We then go on to discuss what clients and coach do in this stage, offering a sequence of steps that may be taken in the coaching session. We end with some suggested coaching tools.

What Is a Dream?

In Appreciative Coaching, creating a dream is a conscious, deliberate process. We choose the word *dream* over others for two reasons. First, it draws on more than twenty years of successful Appreciative Inquiry change efforts to help people in organizations imagine a more inspiring, positive, and life-giving future for themselves. Second, the word *dream* has a broad connotation of envisioned images, voices, metaphors, symbols, and other feelings experienced either during sleep or as part of a conscious effort to anticipate the future. Although we know that the unconscious and subconscious play a role in that mysterious process we call dreaming,[1] for our purposes we focus only on intentional, wakeful dreaming that involves anticipatory images and reality, positive affect, and generative metaphor. In defining the Dream Stage, we occasionally use the term *vision*, which is also employed by AI in organizational visioning.

Anticipatory Images and Reality

Like dreaming, creating images of one's potential appears to be a natural human process that has both physical and psychological explanations and consequences. As we have seen in our discussion of the Anticipatory Principle in Chapter Four, there is a strong connection between positive image and positive action. Cooperrider proposes that human systems have an innate heliotropic tendency—that is, "an observable and largely automatic tendency to evolve in the direction of positive anticipatory images of the future."[2] In his use of "heliotropic" he draws an analogy with the many kinds of plants that exhibit a tendency to grow in the direction of sunlight—their life-giving force. Coaches in sports have long made use of this tendency and of the connection between image and action by helping athletes imagine peak performances before playing.[3]

We now know that self-initiated imagery has consequences that are often indistinguishable from their genuine sensory counterparts; that is, mind and body appear to function as a unified interdependent system.[4] For example, studies have shown that just anticipating or imagining a hostile encounter can raise a person's blood pressure as much as the encounter itself.[5]

Anticipating the future seems to guide people toward that future—be it negative or positive in nature. Perhaps the time dimension of the future—which some refer to as "anticipatory reality"—functions as a predominant force in the dynamic of all images.[6] In other words, people are somehow always involved in anticipating the future.

Positive Affect

From the appreciative perspective, positive affect also plays a key role in dreaming. After all, we want our clients to be creative in their imagery of the future, and we know from the Positive Principle that positive emotions expand on human capabilities. Cooperrider reviewed research in the areas of the placebo effect, the Pygmalion effect, and positive emotion, all of which demonstrated the power of positive imagery in creating future reality.[7] Most of us are familiar with the placebo effect, a process in which a positive belief in the effectiveness of a remedy triggers a healing response that is just as powerful as conventional treatment. This effect demonstrates the direct link between positive image and positive action: positive imagery can awaken the body to its own self-healing powers.[8]

Research on the Pygmalion effect[9] has demonstrated the impact that the positive image of others can have on an individual or group. It appears that humans behave toward others in ways that are congruent with their beliefs about the others. This suggests that coaches may play a significant role in supporting the future dreams of their clients with genuine positive affect. As we've seen in previous chapters, positive emotions, such as hope, joy, interest, and contentment, are important in helping create a heightened feeling of optimism about the future.[10]

Generative Metaphor

Metaphors are ways of transferring understanding and meaning from one area into another. They organize people's perceptions and serve as a framework for them to see similarity between two seemingly unrelated objects or experiences. In the literary context, Shakespeare was well known for his metaphors, such as this popular one: "All the world's a stage, and all the men and women in it, merely players."[11]

Since the 1970s, metaphors, especially generative metaphors, have played an increasingly significant role in helping various disciplines cope with complex issues—from physics and global governance to education, organizations, and psychotherapy.[12] In the area of policymaking, urban planner Donald Schön was instrumental in demonstrating that metaphors shape people's perceptions and understanding of social situations and that often people are unaware of metaphors that underlie their decision-making processes; in fact, he asserted that people tend to frame social problems in terms of metaphors.[13]

In the organizational context, Barrett and Cooperrider point out that the use of generative metaphor is growing in popularity as a transformative way to see the world with new eyes.[14] They describe a metaphor as being generative when it "deliberately fosters formation of new impressions and judgments" which then give birth to new meanings.[15] Thus, new metaphors can help shift people's images or perceptions, which in turn can change their experiences. Generative metaphors can become catalysts for helping individuals explore new opportunities unconstrained by the past[16] and can facilitate learning and help construct new social reality.[17] We have seen that generative metaphors help some clients create new scenarios for their future and overcome the effects of fear and doubt.

Máirín was a client who had a penchant for using generative metaphors to help her move forward. When she and her coach first started talking about her dream, which was to live her own life, she immediately saw herself and her life as four piles of playing cards. Each of the four piles represented some aspect of herself that she needed to "play." She named each pile with one word: work, relationships, health, and spirit. Her work pile represented her formal social role and her responsibility to model wholeness to others. Her relationships pile included things she enjoyed doing, whether they were socializing, being in nature, or taking downtime. Her health pile represented things she needed to do for herself, such as exercising and eating well. The spirit pile represented guidance and was a reminder that she was in good company and connected with

God and nature. She wanted to be playing all of the cards so she could be whole and in balance, and could live her own life.

Wendy was another client who saw her future in metaphorical images. One image was that of a blue bird with a large wingspan flying in circles much like a person doing somersaults and figure eights in the air. Another image was of a flowing river. She saw these metaphors as relating to the energetic flow of spirit and creativity in her life. They generated a new view for her—to remain connected to the essence and energy of life and to have her work revolve around the flow of this energy. She expressed how these metaphors helped her better understand the ebb and flow of other people's energy and creativity and how she could use her energy and skills to reach out in her marketing and work.

In our effort to capture the holistic and metaphorical nature of the Dream process, we also found kinship with the Dreamtime beliefs of the Australian Aboriginal people. In both their waking lives and their art, the indigenous people of Australia use the metaphor of dream to understand their own existence and their relationship to the environment. They believe that they are descended from ancestors who rose through the crust of the earth from Dreamtime and who created all the natural things of their landscape—trees, rocks, rivers, and people. To the native people, all things are related through their beginnings, and all are equally sacred. Dreamtime is depicted in Aboriginal paintings, which often use immense, darkly painted canvases, giving the impression of night or caves (perhaps the innards of the earth), with overlaid colored dots to symbolize animals, plants, people, and other objects.

Many of the Aboriginal paintings in the art museums of Sydney and Melbourne have an otherworldly quality, as if the viewer were walking into their Dreamtime. When native guides take visitors on a walkabout (what Australians call a hike) at the Aboriginal sacred site of Uluru, better known to Westerners as Ayers Rock, they talk about the land and the nomadic nature of their people by using dream language, connecting themselves to the tufted scrub and the indentations in the rock's face as if these objects were their conscious equals. They live in and with a spirit world that is integrated into their wakeful lives, in a current Dreamtime.

As Appreciative Coaches, we were drawn to the holistic quality of Aboriginal dreaming as it is not separate from the wakeful world, but integrated into it. Perhaps Dreamtime is a metaphor for the connection between our deepest longings, our spirit, and the action we take toward that longing. We do not believe that the Dream Stage is linear in its structure. We would expect, from a holistic time perspective, that our dreams spring from the experiences, hopes, and desires of our past, present, and future.

As Appreciative Coaches, we seek to make full use of our clients' capacity to dream in its broadest form. The Dream Stage in the Appreciative Coaching process is thus distinct from the more traditional process of defining a goal. Dream may encompass the environmental, social, and spiritual forces that affect a client. It is sometimes slow to make itself known due to shifting elements, images, and insights. So long as a client is determined to make a preferred future come to life, a dream for us is not fantasy, nor is it delusion.

The Coach's Focus in the Dream Stage

In the Dream Stage, client and coach build on the exploration of the Discovery Stage. They attend to what the client reports about his interior landscape: the storytelling of past achievements, the acknowledgment of talents and abilities, and the assertion of longings. These explorations have sown seeds that can be nurtured into a coherent landscape in the Dream Stage. Some clients may have a picture of the future already in mind; for others, creating a dream may be a novel experience. In either case, the client creates a dream by first learning about himself, then creating images of his possibilities, and finally giving voice to his longings for his future. The Dream Stage has an iterative quality; that is, coach and client may weave back and forth between Discovery and Dream, or may move forward to Design only to return to Dream. Some dreams take shape and evolve over lifetimes. As coaches, we need to be sensitive to the iterative nature of the creation of dreams and move at each client's unique pace and rhythm. As shown in Figure 7.1, the coach's job in the Dream Stage is threefold:

1. Encouraging the client to create images of possibilities
2. Inviting the client to give voice to her preferred future
3. Affirming the client's dream

First, the coach helps the client bring together the learnings about the topic that the client has brought to the coaching relationship and encourages him to create images of possibilities for his future. Second, the coach works with the client to give voice to these possibilities in the shape of the dream itself. Giving voice means to bring the dream into a coherent form. And third, throughout the entire stage, the coach provides affirmation to the client that he can dream big and make his greatest desires known. The following is an example of how a client might move from Discovery into Dream.

Figure 7.1. Dream

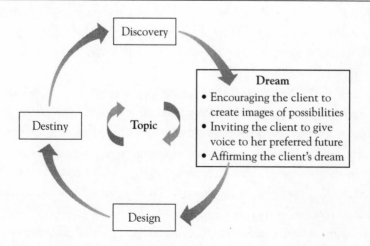

Diane's Story

Diane, a vibrant and energetic saleswoman in her early sixties, came to coaching with two goals: to restore balance to a very unbalanced life (most of it was spent working) and to find more intimacy for herself (in a romantic relationship or deepening friendships). Diane and her coach launched into the Discovery process with the topic of balance and intimacy, and Diane began to make strides when her work situation changed for the better. She took a new job that allowed her work-free hours in the evening. Her days had more space in them, she could go to bed at a reasonable hour, and she had more energy. When this occurred, a longtime dream again popped to the forefront of the coaching relationship.

Diane's dream was to support couples during their separation and divorce, using all that she had learned during her own divorce twenty years earlier. She wanted to help individuals remain whole and positive and learn from each other while they went through the process of dissolving their marriage. She had tried several times to realize her dream, but without success. Despite a work background as a mediator and qualifications as a couples' consultant, she was unable to make the transition from sales to the kind of role she had dreamed of.

Her coach realized that the threads of this dream had already emerged as part of the Discovery process. Diane had talked about the positive path she had followed for herself in recovering from divorce and maintaining a positive relationship with her ex-spouse, and about the experience and knowledge she had gained over the years as a mother, wife, and ex-wife. She longed to share her positive experiences with others when she saw the pain that divorce caused them.

At first, Diane was hesitant about pursuing her dream yet again, unsure whether she had the energy to try. But through appreciative and dream-oriented questions, her coach helped Diane focus on how she felt when she was at her best and what helping role would best allow her past strengths, skills, and successes to shine. Then, both her coach and Diane had a "blinding glimpse of the obvious": Diane could become a coach herself, as coaching was an excellent match for her positive approach to helping others. Diane saw coaching as something that would allow her to get

the training she needed, to work in the profession toward certification, and
to continue employment as a salesperson for as long as she needed to.

All clients are unique in how they approach the Dream Stage. The Appreciative Coaching approach was successful in helping Diane overcome her disappointment and reluctance over past attempts to change. Diane's coach focused on giving Diane a more positive foundation on which to take risks and provided her with much positive affect to help her build on the positive emotions she needed to generate excitement and belief in her possibilities.

Encouraging the Client to Create Images of Possibilities

Our gentle insistence on framing stories positively in Discovery eventually engages most clients in articulating a dream. We help them do this by encouraging them to reflect on what they learned in the Discovery Stage, to declare what it is they desire, and to form images or statements of possibilities in their future. We don't expect our clients to leap into a future that is disconnected from their past and from who they are as individuals. To do so would be to create a fantasy rather than a dream grounded in personal history.

As Appreciative Coaches, we ask clients to be reflective and courageous and to go for the things that move them—those things that elicit their passion. The Positive and Anticipatory Principles come into play when the coach asks the client to create images of what his life would look, feel, be, and function like if those exceptional moments and the life-giving properties of his past and present became the norm rather than the exception.[18]

Sometimes, images of possibilities come into view more quickly or clearly for the coach than for the client. When this happens, the Anticipatory Principle reminds coaches that the most important resource we have for helping clients generate their desired future is the collective imagination and conversation. Our lives (coaches' and clients') are continually being coauthored. So on the occasions when the client may need some encouragement to clearly express aspects of a longed-for future, the coach can help her see even more broadly to other possibilities by referring to those markers of potential indicated by talents, actions, and successes of the past.

Together, client and coach can list past accomplishments, identify patterns of peak performance, and focus on the client's best moments. They can also look at activities the client enjoys regardless of expertise, and talk about role models or people most admired, to see what resonates with the client. In essence, the coach helps the client realize and embrace his multiple possibilities.

Máirín, the client who saw herself and her life as four stacks of playing cards, was feeling overwhelmed by her obligations. She started coaching so she could begin creating some order and balance in her life. She worked in the family business, where she and her siblings managed the company. Her position as head of human resources, although important to the company, was not strongly valued by some of her siblings. When she started coaching, she was putting in sixty hours a week at work and had just added a community commitment that would raise that number to seventy hours. She realized there was little distinction between her life and the family business. She felt generally underappreciated and strangely absent from her own life.

Máirín and her coach talked about what she really wanted to be doing and what she could get rid of to give her some immediate relief. In Discovery, they focused on her strengths and accomplishments. Máirín became clear about what she wanted: to learn how to make herself a priority. She didn't have enough downtime or personal time. Her work life often left her without energy or opportunity to be more social. She felt obliged to spend much time with her family, which further depleted her. She needed support in building a life that included her own needs. She was willing to make substantial changes and was very focused on results.

Máirín began to create a dream for herself: that her life would become her own. It was a big vision that had an impact on her whole person—her work, her self-image, her values, and her desires for a different future. But she was at a crossroads. She could continue living life largely for others, or she could begin living her own life from the inside out. Máirín worked with her coach to form images of possibilities in her life. She did this by identifying time for herself, gaining respect and appreciation at work, taking good care of herself, and building more positive feelings and experiences into her life.

As in Máirín's situation, sometimes it is necessary for the coach to help the client go beyond limitations of the past to see other possibilities. Some clients come to coaching from a long family history of being told they're not okay, or they may have been taught that speaking about success is boastful and wrong. Such learnings from the past may have set up limitations around what our clients dare to believe about themselves. In these cases, the coach can help engage the client's capacity to access more positive memories rather than negative ones and to perceive ambiguous situations for their positive rather than negative qualities.[19]

In working with such clients, we need to appreciate the courage required from them to declare their possibilities. Believing in our clients and offering them positive emotional support can inspire them and give them hope to reinterpret their past. We may need to hold the dream for our clients—that is, hold firm to the belief that they can and will "move toward the generative and creative images that reside in their most positive core—their values, visions, achievements, and best practices."[20]

Inviting the Client to Give Voice to Her Preferred Future

Forming images of possibilities into a dream is an organic and dynamic process that continues through one's lifetime. In Appreciative Coaching, we have the privilege of working with clients for a defined period of time to help them integrate possibilities for their future into a coherent picture. We invite them to imagine a life in which those special moments of exceptional vitality found in their stories become the norm rather than the exception.[21] We want our clients to make conscious choices about what they desire in their future, and we engage in dialogue with them to help them uncover their deeper wishes and hidden possibilities. We ask such questions as

- What is the world calling for you to be?

- What are the most enlivening and exciting possibilities for you?

- What is the inspiration for your life?[22]

We want to help them give voice to their preferred future in a way that pushes their creative edge. Their picture of the future may be composed of three types of images: a prophetic image, a poetic image, and a normative image.[23] A prophetic image encapsulates their expectancies and beliefs about the future. It comes from a deep inner knowledge of what they believe will come about. This image acts much like a positive self-fulfilling prophecy. A poetic image depicts imagined possibilities or alternatives for the future. Like the Poetic Principle, it reminds people of the multiple inter-pretations of their lives and of the array of potential choices they have. Finally, the normative image contains ideological or value-based images of what should be. People's deepest values and beliefs are held in these images.

Through "possibility conversations," we ask clients to wonder about their greatest desires. We invite them to think great thoughts and generate a picture of an inspiring future that encompasses or is integrated into many aspects of their lives.

Máirín's coach began asking her questions about giving voice to her future—What was the world calling her to be? What inspired her? This process led Máirín to recognize what she already knew: that she possessed strong leadership qualities. She was insightful, highly intelligent, capable of visionary foresight, and compassionate and understanding with others. She had an easy way with people and had great analytical abilities. She was recognized as a leader in the community, and her abilities were used behind the scenes in the family business. To her coach, it seemed that a key step for Máirín to take in leading her own life was to claim her lead-ership abilities.

But Máirín seemed caught on the horns of her own dilemma—stay safe behind the scenes and subject herself to unwanted influences, or step forward and become the "prophetic" image of herself she thought she kept well hidden from others. Perhaps invisibility would have worked, except that others had already seen her capabilities (as is so often the case), and she was inexorably drawn to realize her potential.

Her coach could see that the cost of the struggle within Máirín was taking its toll. One of the tipping points, however, was Máirín's strong belief in her own values—her normative image of herself. She felt morally, ethically, and spiritually bound to tell the truth and have integrity with others. This need to demonstrate integrity with others provided great leverage in the coaching relationship because ultimately Máirín realized she had to apply that same integrity to herself.

It is helpful to encourage clients like Máirín to express an image of the future in a "concrete" way—that is, to help them express their dream in a manner that gives it some substance and makes it more real. When a client concretizes his dream by sharpening its image and making clear his expectations about it, he actually directs his mind to create what he has imagined.

How a client depicts his dream varies depending on his natural inclinations, styles, and talents. Alan wrote down his dream, mostly in the form of bulleted items. He enjoyed organizing his thoughts in this way and connecting them much like a mind map. Susanna simply named her coming year as "the year to come into my own." For her, this summarized the notes she took as she and her coach discussed her dream and encapsulated it. She found that by giving the coming year a title, she could keep her dream constantly in mind. Wendy asked a friend to take her through a guided meditation. This method freed her mind to express images that she enjoyed interpreting. There are many other ways to bring form to a dream: creating a mandala or a collage of pictures works well for some people, as does identifying a generative metaphor, as Máirín did with her playing cards.

What is common to all these techniques is our request to clients to describe their dream to us in an active voice and in the present tense, so it feels as if it were already manifest.

Affirming the Client's Dream

The coach's stance must be one of belief and support in two areas: that the client's dream is legitimate and that the client can indeed realize her dream. As we mentioned with regard to the Pygmalion effect, people respond to the positive images that others have of them.[24] As coaches, we affirm that our clients are capable and competent and that they can and will achieve their dreams. A coach's positive attitude and connection with the client will influence her belief in herself and her ability to make long-term changes. This "affirmative capacity," this ability to tune into the positive aspects of another human being, is truly "a remarkable human gift."[25]

Máirín's sense of integrity cemented her decision to pursue a big vision for herself. Her dream was to create her own life. She would know it was her own life if it included having time for herself, being respected and appreciated at work, taking good care of herself, and building more positive feelings and experiences into her daily life. The next step in the Dream Stage was for Máirín's coach to begin supporting and sharing Máirín's feeling that her dream was not only legitimate but inevitable and that she could realize it. It took great courage for Máirín to choose the path of her dream, and her coach felt privileged to accompany her on that journey.

We coach our clients to dream big by helping them move toward their highest and most desired ideals. It is important to help clients create expansive dreams because, as Cooperrider notes, dreams contain an inherent paradox.[26] No matter how big a person's ideals may be, they present him with built-in limits. He is restricted by their boundaries and the boundaries of his imagination and beliefs. Therefore, to assist our clients in achieving the most they can, we help them dream as big as they can. And to support them in daring to dream big, we help them remember their talents, abilities, and successes and help them see how these enduring traits will be with them in the future.

A Coaching Sequence in the Dream Stage

Although there is no template for a session in the Dream Stage, there is a typical flow to how the process unfolds. In moving into the Dream Stage, the client reviews her learnings from Discovery, acknowledging those strengths and aspirations that fit with her desired future. The coach helps the client expand her thinking about possibilities and create a positive focus and anticipation for the dream. Finally, the coach helps the client envision her dream or picture of the future and to make a firm declaration for it. The client and coach typically follow this sequence:

1. The client acknowledges her aspirations and strengths.

2. The client and coach anticipate her dream.

3. The client declares her dream.

Step One: The Client Acknowledges Her Aspirations and Strengths

The transition into Dream requires the coach to gently turn the client's attention to those aspirations he would like to fulfill and those strengths and skills about which he is confident in the present. The client may also share what it would feel like to fulfill these aspirations (for example, joy in achieving an educational degree, relief at finding a smaller place to live, happiness at selling a first novel).

Karen had started with her company as a college intern. Her strengths at that time were ambition, careful attention to detail, and the tenacity to stick with projects until they were completed. As the company expanded, Karen's role and responsibilities changed from those of intern, to programmer, to supervisor, to midlevel manager. She married and had a child, which also added to her many responsibilities. Her request for coaching came when she realized that her past strengths were no longer enough. She felt mired in a tangle of details that reduced her ability to be an effective manager, mother, and wife. So Karen and her coach talked about new strengths underlying some of her more recent successes. Karen was surprised to find that she had a fearless commitment to her own change process and aspired to create a more positive and relaxed future for herself.

Step Two: The Client and Coach Anticipate Her Dream

In this step, coach and client work to expand the client's thinking about her possibilities and to create enough positive affect and anticipation to help her move forward. The coach asks questions that help the client give voice to her preferred future. Questions about what inspires her, what excites her, or what she sees as her true potential, mission, or purpose in life are all means to expand the client's thinking and generate momentum. Some clients respond readily to this process and find it stimulating; others might see the questions as challenging or difficult to answer.

Clients who have been long separated from their true feelings or desires often cannot easily recognize them. As Appreciative Coaches, we are sensitive to the fact that the individual client's frame of reference sets the pace and rhythm of the coaching relationship, as we discussed in Chapter Five. When clients have difficulty imagining positive possibilities, we have found it helpful to focus on increasing the amount of positive feeling and positive self-talk they can incorporate into their daily lives. When we have seen them make this shift, we have been inspired by their empowered perspective.

Karen's coach asked her to imagine all the possibilities Karen would like to have available to help her live a more relaxed and stress-free life— one in which she had time to do her job well and attend to her family and friends. Her coach provided Karen with lots of affirmation for her early successes with the company, the amount of respect and support her boss showed her, and her husband's and friends' support of her in creating new habits. Bolstered by this consistent reminder of her capabilities, Karen began to see herself learning organizational skills from her boss, the ability to "let go" from her husband, and time management tips from her friends. She saw a network of people helping her create a more relaxed yet organized professional and social environment for herself.

Step Three: The Client Declares Her Dream

In the third step, the client is ready to articulate a dream based on the possibilities he has generated. Some dreams are grand and sweeping; others may be specific and focused. There is no "right" form for a dream to take—dreams are unique, holistic, generative descriptions of the future that are rich with possibility, emotion, inspiration, excitement, hope, and often some fear. If they are big, they may take some time to unfold, as in Máirín's case. If they come readily to mind, they may be realized quickly. Coaches can use an array of questions to pique the interest of clients (see Questions in the Coaching Tools in the Dream Stage section). The importance of this step is the tangible declaration the client makes for her dream (for example, in a picture, an affirmation to another person, a written statement, or a metaphorical story).

Karen declared her dream as finding increased effectiveness and relaxation in her life. Once she accepted this vision as possible, she began shifting her priorities. It was as if the anticipated image of herself as more relaxed allowed her to effectively prioritize her current responsibilities. She had created another view of herself—a person who enjoyed her multiple roles in life and had the determination, tenacity, and commitment to take care of herself. In her new vision of living a more relaxed life, she saw herself using her skills and strengths to attend to details in a productive, life-enhancing way. She no longer worried over unimportant details that did not contribute to her well-being or to that of her family or employer. By letting these details go, she would find time to add some of the pleasures she had enjoyed before assuming the roles of manager, wife, and mother.

Coaching Tools in the Dream Stage

We began this chapter by stating that coaches from different traditions all have ways to help their clients dream and that there are many fine tools available with these various approaches. In this section, we highlight some categories that may spark ideas for finding or creating tools to positively engage clients in the process of generating their dream.

Questions

In the Dream Stage, we like to ask appreciative questions that help point clients in the direction of a future desire or ideal. We like hearing clients describe a future where they are more satisfied, more peaceful, and more fulfilled. They may respond with what they will be doing or how they will feel. In any case, we want to solicit a positive view of their desired future. Here are some sample questions:

- Jump into the future (one year, five years, ten years . . .). What do you see? What are you doing? Who are you with? Where are you living? What are you excited about?

- If you could have three wishes, what would they be?

- Thinking about the times you were most happy, what about these times would you want to carry into the future?

- Looking into the future, who are you called to be? What work are you called to do?

- What do you notice about yourself when you dream of your future?

- If you could communicate with yourself in the future, what questions would you want to ask yourself? What would you like others to ask of you?

- What would your mentor (mom, grandmother, best friend, fairy godmother) wish for you in your future?

It can also be helpful to clients to coax out the details of their dreams by following up with specific questions. For example, if a client's dream is of a thriving consulting practice in medical technology serving international customers, the questioning might begin with "What are you doing specifically in your practice that brings you great joy? How do your customers describe the quality of your work? What are they telling others that they really like about your work?" Similar questions can apply to the work environment: "What is going on in your office, your home, or the office of your customer in this dream?" All of these are intended to elaborate on the dream so that it is as clear as if it were a present reality.

The Expression of Dreams

Some clients find writing a powerful way to share their dream because it causes them to choose words and create descriptions that attend to the nuances of what they desire. Other clients find words too limiting or writing too linear and prefer to use pictures as their medium. Still others prefer finding symbols or using metaphors to represent the totality of their dream. Our role as coaches is to help clients find the way to express their dream that is most meaningful for them.

However clients choose to depict their dreams, we do ask them to share their visions with us. One of the necessary steps leading from anticipation to reality is for clients to give voice and attention to what they would like to create. It is important that they declare their future intentions to others, who will then help hold their dream while it comes to fruition. To this end, we like to encourage clients to tell their stories of the future in lavish detail. Imagery is a significant part of learning, and it assists our clients in the next stages of designing their future and sustaining their destinies.

One of the essential aspects of bringing any dream or vision into reality is our clients' excitement as they create and anticipate their preferred future. The more they can feel what it is they want—especially positive feelings about themselves and what it is they would like to achieve—the faster it manifests.

Summary

Following exploration in the Discovery Stage, clients move to the Dream Stage. The purpose of this stage is to help clients articulate a meaningful picture of the future they choose. To aid them, we help clients generate images of possibilities in which they have some investment of positive feeling and desire. We then invite them to give voice to what they would like to bring from the present into the future and what they would most like to create in the future. Finally, we do what we can to affirm their dream and hold it in a positive time and space during its fruition.

Creating a dream is a deliberate process that includes the elements of anticipatory images and reality, positive affect or feeling, and generative metaphor in the expression of the dream. There is a clear connection between positive, anticipatory images and positive action. Positive affect also plays a key role in creating energy and optimism about the future. A generative metaphor can provide the means for clients to make transformative changes by shifting their current perceptions to what they imagine the future can be. Dreams can be symbolic or metaphorical; they offer a way for clients to proceed from what is known to what is yet to be known.

We presented a coaching sequence that involves three typical steps used in this stage: the client describes his aspirations and strengths, the coach and client anticipate the dream, and the client declares the dream.

We described two coaching tools: questions and the expression of dreams. As always, appreciative language is important in this stage as coach and client work to uncover the client's true desires about the future and to ensure there is enough positive feeling for her to venture into the unknown.

8

Design Stage

Directing Attention and Action

Everyone designs who devises courses of action aimed
at changing existing situations into preferred ones.
Herbert Alexander Simon (1916–2001), Nobel laureate

A ll of us are both the designers of our world and the product of
our own designs."[1] This reference to the Design Stage in
Appreciative Inquiry applies with equal significance to Appreciative
Coaching. This third stage of the Appreciative Coaching process is
about helping clients direct their attention and take action so that
they become the designers of the future they most desire. We know
as Appreciative Coaches how important it is for clients to influence
their own destiny by making choices and acting in ways that
reflect their most positive core and their desired future. As we stated
before, we try to help our clients change their mental model of how
the world works from that of a fixed and determined machinelike universe to one that is open, dynamic, interconnected, and full of living
qualities.[2] This view of the universe supports them in their change
and supports the purpose of the Design Stage, which is to provide a
foundation and structure for clients to proactively attain their dream.

In Chapter Seven, we saw how the creation of dreams can be a
fascinating and inspirational process as we watch our clients articulate a meaningful picture of a future of their own choosing. Dreams
come in different sizes and levels of complexity. The larger and

bolder the dream, the more likely that its realization will be distant in the future. The more immediate or specific the dream, the more rapidly it may manifest. It is that period of time between the artic-ulation of the dream and its manifestation that is the focus of the Design Stage. Occasionally, the time between the creation of a dream and its fulfillment can seem long.

In some ways our clients are like explorers of their own future ter-ritory. The trip toward the dream holds great excitement, meaning, and desire, but our clients can't predict the adventures they'll have during the journey nor the circumstances of their arrival. Like successful ship captains who make sure they have accurate maps, appropriate naviga-tional tools, loyal crew, and sufficient provisions, clients need to pre-pare themselves with the right tools to guide them on their way.

So it is with this journey in mind that we support clients in the Design Stage by preparing for this exciting passage. We want them to be proactive and travel with a sense of direction and energy, but we do not want them to be so overwhelmed by their dreams that they are immobilized. We support clients in sustaining their focus, making choices, and taking actions.

A word of caution: designing for the future is not about creat-ing detailed action plans, as is commonly understood in traditional planning approaches. They can actually restrict clients from taking advantage of the multiple opportunities and choices that are sure to cross their path. A focus that is too detailed tends to limit clients to re-creating the present and seeing only what is immediately in front of them. Our clients' lives are much more fluid, dynamic, and unpredictable than specific action plans can account for. We prefer to give them the opportunity to think in broad strokes, to stretch and then to act toward their desired future.

The Coach's Focus in the Design Stage

The coach's focus in the Design Stage is to help the client create a foundation and structure for attaining her dream. During this period of transition, the client needs to design a path that values, prizes, and honors where she is today and that mobilizes action and sustains momentum. As shown in Figure 8.1, in the Design Stage, the coach works with the client to ground her vision or dream by helping her with three activities:

1. Assisting the client in bringing the dream into focus
2. Affirming the reality of the dream
3. Supporting mindful choices and actions

One of the key supportive actions Appreciative Coaches take in this stage is to engage in positive dialogue with clients about their dream and its realization. We ask questions to clarify and add meaning, probe for specifics, affirm their potential, encourage experimentation, empathize when the going gets tough, support their efforts, and hold them accountable for their actions and decisions. Dialogue with our clients can be fateful, as we saw in our discussion of the Constructionist Principle. Our clients are continually creating meaning and reality through their communication and language with others, and we can play a significant role

Figure 8.1. Design

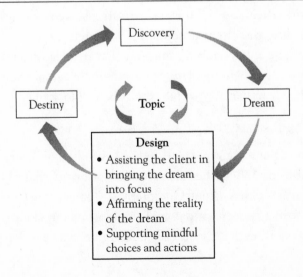

in helping them move from imagining a tenuous dream to actually manifesting it.

It is not a path lightly trod, however. As Appreciative Coaches, we understand that although we have no control over the ease or difficulty of clients' journeys into the future, we are their partners, ever vigilant and supportive when they turn to us for reassurance or help. This stage is the most challenging for coach and clients. It is a journey of learning and change on the part of clients, who may move forward only to find themselves slipping backwards. It is an unfolding that may happen quickly or very slowly. We remind ourselves that we have been invited to accompany them on this path of change. Some clients triumph spectacularly, others partially succeed, and a few give up. For those who reach their dream, we have found a common element: they were willing. They were willing to make substantial changes in their lives to achieve their dream and to take advantage of new awarenesses, opportunities, and support. Only our clients can make the decision to be willing.

Assisting the Client in Bringing the Dream into Focus

There are specific ways the coach can help as the client brings his dream into focus. The first, as we've already mentioned, is through the power of the dialogue the coach has with the client—the language the coach uses and the positive affect she contributes while still holding the client accountable for what he would like to achieve. The coach can be instrumental in two additional ways: she encourages the client to identify priorities for experimentation and helps the client define what future success will look like.

Identifying Priorities

Some dreams are very large. To assist the client in maintaining focus, the coach helps her identify a few priorities that represent major aspects of her dream. Our intent as Appreciative Coaches is to find specific priorities that guide and inspire our clients. They must be priorities that clients can commit to and take action on. In

organizational research studies, one of the reasons certain companies were found to be truly visionary and successful was their practice of setting big challenges for themselves that were so compelling
that they grabbed people in a tangible, energizing, and highly
focused manner. These goals have been described as BHAGs, short-
hand for Big, Hairy, Audacious Goals.[3] Likewise, we know that for
individuals to successfully traverse the sometimes rocky path
between their dream and their future reality, they need to identify
and work on two or three major priorities with characteristics similar to those of BHAGs.

In Chapter Seven, we had a glimpse into Máirín's life and her decision to pursue a big vision for herself—to create her own life. Máirín and
her coach realized that to begin moving toward her dream, Máirín had
some major areas on which to focus. She defined them as taking good care
of herself, building more positive feelings and experiences into her life,
and being respected and appreciated at work. These became the three priorities that helped guide her in creating her own life. They were also compelling enough for her to take action on them.

Defining Success

Once clients have identified their priorities, we ask them to
spend time describing what it looks like when they are successful at
achieving them. Helping clients define what success looks like happens in conversations over time as they begin to work through the
Design Stage.

In Máirín's case, she and her coach began working on what her three
priorities would look like if she were successful at each. To take good care
of herself, Máirín knew she needed to do something, immediately if possible, that would involve more time for herself, for her sleep, for relaxation, and even for play. To become more positive about herself, Máirín
realized she had to focus on ways of bringing more positive affect into her
life, especially in her awareness of positive experiences in her daily life.
Finally, to be respected and appreciated at work, Máirín talked with her
coach about what it would be like to put boundaries around her work and

family relationships. More specifically, they discussed how that would feel to Máirín.

Affirming the Reality of the Dream

There are three ways Appreciative Coaches can help affirm the reality of their clients' dream. First, they help them bring their preferences to life. We talked about clients giving voice to their dream. This is a continuation of that process to ensure that clients voice their wants and needs as they actualize their dream. They may need to ask others for information or feedback, request a favor, or take the time to truly understand what they are trying to achieve.

Next, Appreciative Coaches help clients leverage their core positive beliefs and values to sustain them through the change process. We've had clients who declare their positive intentions for the year or name a theme for the year to add gravity to their commitment to their dream and priorities. We encourage these actions because such declarations and commitment can be made only by those individuals who have changed their stance from one of resignation about their life to one of possibility.[4] The idea is to help clients engage their own capacity for change and create synergistic interactions with others. Third, coaches affirm and appreciate clients wherever they are in the Design Stage. As we stated before, we question, encourage, support, and also hold them accountable.

Máirín's health was her first concern, so she and her coach began with a focused concentration on self-care, which included taking time for herself, recognizing and legitimizing her feelings, and focusing on her physical and mental well-being. Getting enough sleep, relaxing, and learning to bring play and spontaneity into her daily life were commitments to herself that Máirín and her coach agreed were very important. Máirín eventually took care of all her health needs, going to doctors and seeing health care professionals—things she had put off for years. Then Máirín made a grand gesture for herself, which surprised her coach. She bought a sports car, which she had always wanted and which gave her a heady sense of freedom. It helped strengthen her positive core because she gave herself

permission to make that decision and did not need anyone's approval for
such a joyous act.

Eventually, at the suggestion of her coach, Máirín began recording
her accomplishments and projecting what she wanted to accomplish in the
coming year related to her priorities. She then decided to make a declara-
tion for herself—to carry herself with dignity and grace. She later created
a theme for the year: "Focus on myself first." Throughout this process
with Máirín, her coach knew what to focus on (her three priorities) but
had little clarity or foresight on how Máirín's path forward would unfold.
However, she never doubted that Máirín would realize her dream if she
remained committed and willing.

Supporting Mindful Choices and Actions

Clearly, one of the coach's roles in the Design Stage is to ensure that
the client makes mindful choices and commits to meaningful
actions. In this stage, we encourage clients to take actions and use
experimentation to move themselves forward. Action is at the base
of all coaching methodologies, and Appreciative Coaching is no
exception. But mindful choices must precede action. We like to
guide our clients to be deciders first, then doers. In that way, their
action is thoughtful and reflective and part of a bigger picture.
There are two specific ways we support our clients in their choices
and actions: encouraging them to enjoy the moment and making
sure they engage supporters.

Enjoying the Moment

Although it may seem that the focus of the Design Stage is
mostly on the future, it is actually on the present. Our clients' lives
are in the now, so we want them to enjoy their journey and savor
the present moment. This awareness of the now can work to our
clients' advantage as they become attentive to what life is offering
them in the creation of their dream. We also support clients in
enjoying the moment by identifying occasions where through new
behaviors and new applications of skills or talents, they can easily

try out and validate aspects of the new dream. Identifying these opportunities helps them renew their energy when an experiment seems to fail.

Engaging Supporters

Humans are social beings who love, play, and learn through interactions with others. Clients benefit when they ask others to support them in designing their dream. When they share a dream, they share a picture, and the picture stimulates others to ask questions and share their own ideas. Others may even have new or different interpretations of the dream that draw on new talents or desires. Such interaction can help define the dream more clearly and bring new opportunities to the fore. Because sharing a dream, identifying new possibilities, and taking day-to-day actions create their own positive reinforcing cycle, it is important for clients to select supporters who are genuinely affirming. Their positive reinforcement will engender productive energy toward more possibilities and bolder action.

A word of caution is necessary. When clients alter their patterns of behavior or action in the process of moving toward their dream, the changes will affect others around them. For some family and friends, these changes may bring great joy and pride. Others may experience feelings of threat or disappointment and not even realize the origin of those negative feelings. Coaches and clients need to spend some time assessing the quality of clients' support systems. It is helpful for clients to realize that their changes may have an impact on their support system and vice versa.

Máirín's coach saw a crucial part of her task as supporting Máirín in making mindful choices and actions. The three priorities in the Design Stage were improving her self-care, focusing on bringing more positive affect into her life, and putting boundaries around work and family relationships. After beginning with self-care, Máirín and her coach turned immediately to looking at ways of bringing more positive affect into her life. Máirín started observing and attending to her self-talk, pausing to ask herself how she was feeling, and trying to stay in the present rather than reacting to feelings from the past. Her coach asked her to pay attention and give credit to herself every time she chose to do what she really wanted instead of adhering to others' expectations. Máirín came up with her own list of warning signs to signal to herself that she was going back to old habits.

With her coach's guidance, Máirín also focused on learning how to conduct herself professionally at work and set clear boundaries with her family. It required a lot of Máirín's strength and courage to become an advocate for herself and to allow herself to be recognized and praised for her work efforts. Over time, Máirín created a mini-vision of how she wanted to be and look in her work setting—calm, relaxed, composed, and sincere in her dealings with employees and family members. She began taking action and setting an example in the workplace with her professional language and demeanor. She slowly learned gracious ways to say no to the many demands placed on her because of her capabilities. She continually tried to focus on what she wanted to do at work and not on what others thought she should do. Máirín had to set and adhere to boundaries for what she would accept in others' behavior. It was a continual challenge for her, but she pressed forward with increasing success.

Máirín made lots of lists of what she wanted to achieve and recorded her progress at different times. She reported to her coach that she was handling complicated work projects with greater ease and that she now understood the concept of being selective about where she put her attention. She wrote down her achievements for the year, and in every session her coach asked her to report on the positives in her life. Máirín continued designing systems for rewarding herself for positive behavior. She and her coach created another mini-vision for both her personal life and the family business so she wouldn't have to lose one to keep the other.

After creating a theme for the year of focusing on herself first, Máirín decided she was ready to give up the behavior of "propping others up." This change on her part resulted in others more openly acknowledging her true leadership capabilities. She was invited to represent the *family in critical business situations, and family members turned to her for advice and counsel.*

Máirín's journey in the Design Stage was one of courage, commitment, and willingness. Such transformations are not undertaken lightly, and they always involve times of doubt and fear. The coach's role in the Design Stage is to continually affirm the reality of the client's dream and to support the client in the many choices he must make and actions he must pursue.

A Coaching Sequence in the Design Stage

Coaching sessions during the Design Stage can and do take many paths and varied forms. We have therefore found it helpful to identify three key steps that often occur during this stage, as the path forward may be cyclical or iterative in nature. These three steps ensure that the client progresses successfully through this stage, and they serve as a foundation for the coaching process. Whether this stage passes by briefly or more slowly depends on the breadth of the client's dream and the time and resources available to her. The three steps are as follows:

1. The client focuses on compelling priorities.
2. The client reflects on ways in which she is already living the dream.
3. The client takes actions to incorporate elements of the dream into his daily life.

Step One: The Client Focuses on Compelling Priorities

The coach begins by asking the client to identify two or three priorities to focus on, which will give him a way to take structured action toward his dreams. The client may state these priorities in the form of accomplishments to be worked on. The priorities need to be compelling enough to engage the client's commitment and energy.

We met Elizabeth briefly in Chapter Four where her story served as an example of the application of the Poetic Principle. Elizabeth wanted to gain clarity around her life purpose. She was a successful manager in the area of human resource development, but she worked long hours and needed more balance in her personal and work lives. In fact, she felt that her work load was interfering with her ability to clarify her life purpose. She and her coach identified two major priorities in moving forward: self-care and determining what her real passion was. The self-care began immediately with a focus on better management of her time and job responsibilities. Through inquiry about her true passions, Elizabeth recognized that she wanted to help bring out the best in others. She began investigating the profession of coaching as the way to do that and decided that that was her dream—to transition to having her own coaching business. Now Elizabeth's priorities included continued self-care, setting the foundation and structure for a coaching business, and developing a long-term exit strategy from her current position.

Step Two: The Client Reflects on Ways She Is Already Living Her Dream

In this step, the coach asks the client to think of ways in which she may already be living part of her dream. Here the coach encourages the client to recall elements of her dream that may already be in place. Just asking a question about what elements are present can build positive affect. Most clients realize they have past or current successes and strengths in place to support their dream. This realization, in turn, reinforces a cycle of success for them.

Elizabeth's coach asked her what part of her dream she was already living. Surprisingly, Elizabeth responded that she actually had been doing what could be called coaching; she just hadn't thought about it in that way because she was offering her services to colleagues or friends who asked for support in their self-development. As is often the case, Elizabeth was already recognized at work as someone who was able to provide good support and counsel to others because of her integrity and trustworthiness. She was known informally as someone who worked to bring out the best in others.

Step Three: The Client Takes Actions to Incorporate Elements of the Dream into His Daily Life

In this final step, the coach encourages the client to begin manifesting his dream in his daily life. This is the time for making decisions and taking action based on the priorities the client has identified. Which elements of the dream does the client have the energy or desire to begin with? What is most compelling for the client to address? What activity will have the most leverage? Just asking a client to picture his dream fully realized and to identify what daily activities and behaviors he would like to exhibit can be very helpful. As coaches, we sometimes hear themes repeated in the coaching conversations that we can explicitly point out to our clients.

Actions related to self-care are often an immediate focus, as they enable the client to free energy to refocus on what he really wants. Some questions to ask in this stage might be, What can you put in place as support mechanisms? How can you take care of yourself as you embark on this journey? Clients need to make sure they engage others who may be affected by their dream—whether a spouse, children, or fellow employees in a business situation—to gain their support. Clients may also think about other people they trust and value whom they can turn to for support and action on their behalf.

Once Elizabeth settled on the realization of her purpose in life—to help people be the best they could be through coaching—she was filled with energy and determination. Her coach had only to ask questions or make suggestions, and Elizabeth's ideas blossomed. She looked into educational opportunities for coaching. She created a vision of what her coaching business could look like and began to formalize her existing coaching conversations to feel more like a professional. She drafted a coaching brochure and some proposals in order to approach specific organizations to do the type of coaching she was interested in. She and her coach talked about ways she could transition to part-time work. This was a more challenging priority, but it gave Elizabeth an incentive to improve her own self-management. She had to work smarter in order to reach her goal of part-time work. She eventually developed a transition plan to present to her employer and succeeded in that effort. That victory in turn gave her the impetus to enroll in a coach training program. She was on her way!

Coaching Tools in the Design Stage

In this section, we include some tools and techniques to help clients through the Design Stage. As we've noted before, each client is unique, so you will want to choose tools accordingly; some will be more effective than others in engaging a client in identifying and committing to a design for realizing his dream. We hope these ideas are helpful and serve as reminders of other creative approaches. This is the time for coaches to monitor and anticipate the needs of their clients.

Questions

Questions form an important component of the Design Stage, as they do throughout the Appreciative Coaching process. We've listed a few here that may engage clients to think positively about what they need to put in place to make their dreams a reality:

- Thinking about your dream, what would make it come alive for you?

- What in your dream really calls to you, makes you yearn for its fulfillment?

- When you think about your dream, what brings you joy or excitement? What makes you laugh?

- What three big accomplishments would make you feel as though you have come close to your dream?

- What have you done before that you could do again to move toward your future?

- Who are your fellow travelers? Who are people you trust and value who have supported you in the past and will again?

- What do you need to pay attention to so that you feel supported and so that you are taking care of yourself as you embark on this journey?

- What have you already started putting in place? Where is your attention going now as you think about the things you want to do?

- What are small actions that you would like turned into new habits?

- What smaller aspects of your dream could you experiment with now?

- If you were to experiment with one aspect of your dream, what kinds of things can you see yourself trying? How serious is this experiment? How could you make it less serious? More playful?

- If you were to act as if your dream were reality now, what fun would you be having? How could that truly be happening now or in the near future?

- What makes you feel proud and capable today?

The intent of questions in the Design Stage can be varied. The questions may serve to consider the dream both in its totality and in its various aspects, to channel and focus positive energy, to broaden the potential for sustained action toward the dream, and to bring attention to the client's capacity to live the dream in the present.

Mindfulness

In the Design Stage, the coach may choose to work with the client to identify items that the client needs to notice. This tool helps the client name the things he wants so that he will be proactive when faced with unexpected possibilities and offers. Mindfulness does not set a specific goal or action but states an intention to be mindful or attentive. During the course of a day, for instance, it may mean noticing when one is getting tired and then resting or saying yes to an offer of help. In this example, mindfulness merely involves noticing and responding to information that has an impact on self-care. Mindfulness is powerful precisely because it helps the client become aware of and commit to behaviors and actions he would like to see for himself in his desired future.

Máirín was very mindful through the Design Stage in her coaching process. At different times she came up with her own list of warning signs to signal to herself that she was going back to old habits, such as a disheveled office, insufficient sleep, poor eating habits, physical pain, and feelings of being overwhelmed. At other times, she was mindful of making sure that she was using positive self-talk and setting up systems to reward herself for good self-care and setting clear boundaries.

Themes

Another tool we employ in the Design Stage is asking the client to give his year a theme or to name his year. Throughout client-coach discussions in the Discovery and Dream Stages, a theme may emerge that merits a year's focus or that will inspire the client to move concretely toward his dream. For example, after Alan had created his dream for his consulting business, he realized that the coming year was going to be his year "to break out." It was a year that he was going to build his business, be successful in his new marketing strategies, and become known for his work through speaking and writing. He knew this theme was on target because it created a well of energy when he thought about it. The theme was open and broad enough to allow for surprises leading to new actions aligned with his dream.

Susanna identified the year as "coming into my own." Like Alan, she resonated with her theme because it captured her energy and enthusiasm while representing what she wanted to be mindful of each day. They were like code words to her that she had the inner fortitude to feel and present herself as confident, to honor and take care of herself, to use her best skills, and to allow herself to blossom. Máirín created the theme "to focus on herself first" to underscore the importance of self-care and setting boundaries in order to build a life that was her own.

Themes are beneficial until the energy for them fades and the benefits become minimal. Then it may be time for creating a new theme or for moving on to another tool or technique. In our experience a yearly reflection is useful. We often suggest it to clients as a way to create themes and recognize insights that lead to action toward their desired future.

Experimentation for a New Outcome

We introduced experimentation in the Discovery Stage as a tool to help clients explore new behaviors. It gives them a chance to try something new in a nonevaluative context. If the experiment doesn't work, we encourage clients to try something else. It is part of the process of discovering who they are and what they are capable of. It is a safe way for them to stretch and reach beyond the status quo.

In the Design Stage, experimentation has the same connotation, but its purpose is to move clients toward new or different actions and behaviors that they desire to incorporate as part of their future view of themselves. At times, a significant amount of experimentation may be required for clients to make the transition to a different way of acting with or reacting to other people and situations. For example, Máirín spent much time experimenting with ways to set clear boundaries with others that would not be at her own expense. Elizabeth experimented with a number of different strategies to improve how she managed her time as part of her plan to move to part-time employment.

We've found that coaches can benefit their clients most when they watch for opportunities for experimentation, help them construct experiments with the best chance of success, and fully support them whether experiments have a positive or less than satisfactory

outcome. As coaches, we can help clients see all attempts at experimentation as opportunities to gain insight and learn.

Being-With

In Appreciative Coaching, we do not ignore the fact that there are
dark days when clients would like to give up. We recognize this and
work with our clients to address those times. Whatever technique
we choose in doing this, we remember a key tenet of the Positive
Principle: we amplify what we pay attention to. Although we support our clients in acknowledging difficult times, we are careful not
to make their burden heavier.

An effective tool we use to support our clients in these times is
what we term *being-with*. When we use this tool, we acknowledge the
dark emotions. We do not reject them and thereby give them greater
focus. Being-with involves being mindful of emotions and accepting
their presence without judgment. We help a client make use of her
observing self as a way for her to separate from her emotions long
enough to realize that she is more than her feelings. The observing
self may even be able to ask what positive purpose the emotions serve.
For example, if a client is feeling great anxiety before a business meeting, we can help her acknowledge that the meeting does have an element of evaluation and that doing well in this particular meeting is
more important than usual. Therefore, a certain level of anxiety is
not uncommon and may even be useful. Developing the ability to
both observe and act in the same moment can help clients make positive choices as a result of their ability to do these two things at once.

Supporters

Supporters encourage the client to use his best abilities, stay focused,
and keep heart. They also involve others in expressing support.
Whether family, friends, colleagues, counselors, or a combination
thereof, such supporters provide great encouragement, remind the
client of his talents, and applaud his successes; they represent the Positive Principle in action.

A supporter can be anyone the client chooses. Of course, it's preferable for the client to include people who believe in her and who will provide positive support. Our role as Appreciative Coaches is to urge the client first to enlist the support of others and then to encourage her to expand on that number. One technique we use is to ask the client to create a list of the people she knows. To expand her thinking into broader circles, we may ask her to separate the list into categories, such as family and friends, colleagues, and clients. Rather than limiting thinking, the categories prompt the inclusion of many more potential cheerleaders. Once the sorting is complete, the client further divides her lists into *active supporters*, *supporters*, and a *don't know* category. We use the following definitions for these categories:

- *Active supporters:* individuals who have in the past initiated support without clients' asking

- *Supporters:* individuals who clients believe will provide support if they ask

- *Don't know:* individuals whose support is unclear or intermittent

The client can list supporters in a chart similar to Table 8.1, which will allow him to visualize his supporters at a glance. Many clients report that creating the list has made it easier for them to reach out to others in a variety of ways. With the names in front of them, they were able to actively make requests, offers, and simple commitments to many more individuals—something they said they would not have done quite so readily prior to the exercise. As coaches, we help clients identify how they want to connect and interact with each supporter and encourage them to make clear points of contact with these individuals.

Checklist for Forming New Habits

As important as it is to have an image of the future, it is equally crucial to act each day in a manner that is consistent with the dream and the desired direction. The simple steps our clients take every

Table 8.1. Sample List of Supporters

	Active Supporter	Supporter	Don't Know
Family/Friends			
Michael Jones	✓		
Aunt Millie	✓		
Simon Stewart		✓	
Colleagues			
Betty White		✓	
April Millard	✓		
John Donahue			✓
Alex Anjou		✓	
Clients			
Ronald Bedford	✓		
Anton Drew			✓
Carolyn Winnow		✓	

day have a cumulative effect on them and their surroundings. Simple daily actions are the building blocks that bring elements of the future dream into present reality.

To support clients in taking small actions each day, we have found it helpful for them to develop a checklist that identifies items that they would like to see become everyday habits.[5] Although the coach can assist the client in determining the areas most meaningful to her, we find that keeping a simple model in mind helps create a checklist with a balanced focus (see the sample in Table 8.2). We help clients consider aspects of their internal self (for example, beliefs, attitudes, self-talk), their physical self (such as their health, presence, and habits), how they interact with others (for example, support systems, communication skills, norms of behavior), and their environment (such as physical space, e-mail, and services).

Table 8.2. Sample Checklist for Forming New Habits

Daily	Weekly
Internal Self	**Internal Self**
☐ Spend time in reflection	☐ Put week into positive focus
☐ Follow a to-do list	☐ Enjoy quiet/downtime
Physical Self	**Physical Self**
☐ Do morning stretches	☐ Do strength training
☐ Maintain confident stance	☐ Clean car
Interactions with Others	**Interactions with Others**
☐ Make requests clearly	☐ Call mentor
☐ Delegate work	☐ Meet with friends
☐ Respond to e-mail once during day	
Environment	**Environment**
☐ Clear desk at end of day	☐ Bring flowers for office
	☐ File papers

Facing a long checklist can be daunting, so we ask clients to begin by acting on only a few items the first week. Some items may be done daily, others weekly. Each week, clients add only a few entries until they are acting on all items on their checklist each day or week as appropriate.

Summary

The Design Stage is about helping clients build a foundation and structure for attaining their dream. We do that by directing their attention and action in three areas: bringing the dream into focus, affirming the reality of the dream, and supporting mindful choices and actions. This is arguably the most challenging stage for both coach and client. This stage requires that clients exhibit patience, willingness, fortitude, and a belief in themselves. Coaches can provide much positive affect and a parallel belief in the clients' ability to attain their dream.

Dreams come in different sizes and levels of complexity and require varying lengths of time to be realized. There is a general sequence that, if followed, helps the client build the foundation and structure that can support him as he brings his dream to life. First, the client identifies his compelling priorities. Next, the client reflects on the ways in which he is already living his dream. And third, the client makes decisions and takes actions that will begin incorporating the elements of his dream into daily life. Throughout this sequence, the coach assists the client in bringing his dream into focus, affirming the reality of his dream, and supporting his mindful choices and actions toward its fulfillment.

This chapter also described a number of proven tools to work with, including appreciative questions, mindfulness, themes, experimentation for a new outcome, being-with, supporters, and a checklist for forming new habits.

In the next chapter, we move on to the Destiny Stage, our final phase of the Appreciative Coaching model introduced in Chapter Five. This stage is crucial in assisting clients in setting up practices to sustain the realization of their dream.

9

Destiny Stage

Being and Becoming

*Our deepest fear is not that we are inadequate. Our
deepest fear is that we are powerful beyond measure.
It is our light, not our darkness, that most frightens
us. We ask ourselves, Who am I to be brilliant, gor-
geous, talented and fabulous? Actually, who are you
not to be?*

Marianne Williamson, American author
and peace activist, A Return to Love

Destiny was originally titled Delivery by the founders of Appreciative Inquiry (AI), but they increasingly experienced this
designation as not "going far enough" and "not conveying the sense
of liberation" participants experienced in this final stage.[1] They
changed the name of the stage to Destiny to denote a state of being
that encompassed much more than the attainment of goals or the
implementation of designs.

In translating the bigness of Destiny from an organizational setting to an individual one, we see Destiny as enabling brilliance and
the realization of dreams. When developing this stage, we came
across a photograph of a man flinging his arms out to a stunning
sunset. This is Destiny—standing before life and embracing it. People's lives and destinies are always in the process of creation. The

Destiny Stage is not about endings or even beginnings; it is about living one's life fully and well.

Accepting their capacity to create their future can feel immense for clients, and sometimes even frightening. Marianne Williamson writes that people are not really afraid of their inadequacies, but of their own power and light.[2] As Appreciative Coaches, we help clients become aware of their power and acknowledge it. We see glimpses of their light through all the stages of Appreciative Coaching, and we support them in seeing it themselves. Through Discovery, we help clients see their own brilliance and talents more clearly. In Dream and Design, clients enlarge their outlook and courageously stretch toward an engaging future. In Destiny, we help them enjoy the full manifestation of their individual power. The purpose of the Destiny Stage is for clients to internalize and live the reality of their dream—to see their light shining brightly.

The Coach's Focus in the Destiny Stage

The coach's focus in Destiny is fourfold, as shown in Figure 9.1:

Figure 9.1. Destiny

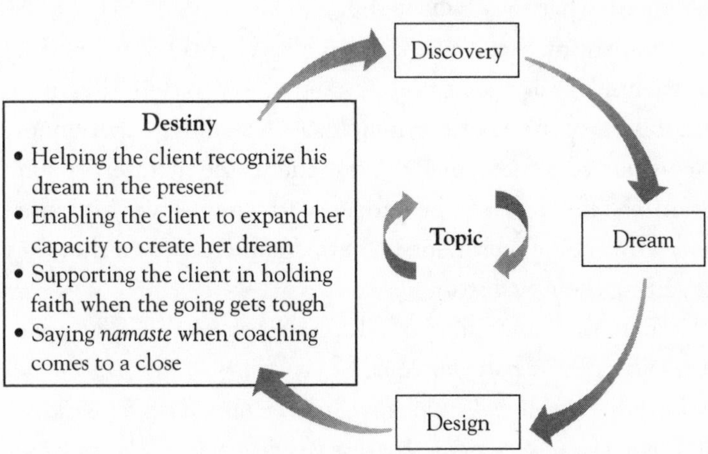

Destiny
- Helping the client recognize his dream in the present
- Enabling the client to expand her capacity to create her dream
- Supporting the client in holding faith when the going gets tough
- Saying *namaste* when coaching comes to a close

Discovery

Topic

Dream

Design

1. Helping the client recognize his dream in the present

2. Enabling the client to expand her capacity to create her dream

3. Supporting the client in holding faith when the going gets tough

4. Saying *namaste* when coaching comes to a close

Helping the Client Recognize His Dream in the Present

Clients generate their dream from their past experiences and successes, their current strengths, and their future desires. Because they integrate their experiences with their desires, they find when they express their dream that they are already living some aspects of it. As they focus on and direct attention to the creation of their dream in Design, they take action toward its realization. Clients may also need to be reminded by the coach of the ways they are already living their dream in the present. By affirming that elements of their dream have already arrived, the coach amplifies the clients' enthusiasm to work toward the dream more energetically—the Positive Principle in action! This in turn encourages clients to extend the boundaries of what they believe they can be.

In the Destiny Stage, we begin to hear clients tell new stories about themselves as they get closer and closer to their dream—a manifestation of the Poetic Principle. As a result of experiencing the appreciative process, many of our clients see themselves quite differently. They learn to be gentler with themselves and more patient with their experiments. They actually recognize that they are rewriting their own stories.

We first told Diane's story in Chapter Seven. An energetic saleswoman in her early sixties, she came into coaching feeling overcommitted in her professional and social life. But a change in her job situation resulted in a new sales position that was less demanding. She found she had more time and energy. This change allowed her longtime dream of coaching couples through separation and divorce to come to the fore. One of her priorities in moving toward her dream was to restore balance in her life by questioning whether each potential activity and relationship would enhance and nurture her life.

As Diane neared the end of her coaching engagement, she recognized the changes she had made. She had slowed down and, in doing so, found that she was focused and able to make better decisions. When her coach asked Diane if she felt she now had more time, she replied, "It's not so much having more time as I'm finding I don't have to rush through a sale as quickly as I had to before. I am calmer in how I do things." This calmness transferred into new efforts toward realizing her dream. While continuing her full-time job, she signed up to take two coaching courses leading to certification in relationship coaching. Early in this course work, she realized she was overloaded and that she really wanted to focus her attention on completing one course well. Instead of carrying her former work pace into this new phase of her life, she decided to drop one of the courses. When her coach noted that Diane could have traded one kind of overload for another, Diane clearly replied, "I am choosing not to do that." She recognized that in her new life she wanted not just more time but more focus.

Reflecting on where the coaching journey began can help clients see the strides they've made. Remembering and celebrating the changes can have a profound effect on clients, giving them confidence and affirming, "It's true. I am living my dream now." Susanna, writing in her final Coaching Prep Form, spoke to how she was already coming into her own:

"In a discussion with unhappy colleagues yesterday, I was reminded again that the way I think about things has changed fundamentally and positively. I am able to reframe in ways that are extremely helpful for me. [My husband] and I went to visit my parents this weekend who live out of town, and it was lovely to be with them. I consciously chose to take some days off and was able to enjoy them fully. I feel much more aware of my strength."

Enabling the Client to Expand Her Capacity to Create Her Dream

In the Destiny Stage of AI, practitioners focus on improving what they call the "improvisational capacity of the organization"[3]; that is, they help organizations demonstrate consistent strength in four key areas of competency or skills: affirmative, expansive, generative, and collaborative.[4] The goal is to help clients build and sustain the capacity to respond and to act quickly and effectively to challenges in an appreciative, positive, integrated manner.

In Appreciative Coaching, we found a parallel for three of these competencies (the last, collaborative, being relevant only in group or organizational contexts). In the Destiny Stage, we want clients to expand their capacity to realize and live their dream, and we help them do this by increasing their skills or competency in the following three areas:

1. *Affirmative competence.* Clients learn to draw on their ability to appreciate their positive possibilities by continuing to focus on their current and past strengths, successes, and potentials. As coaches, we can nurture this affirmative competence in our clients by celebrating their achievements and directing attention to the strengths that are the source of their vitality.

2. *Expansive competence.* Clients are challenged to stretch and move beyond familiar ways of thinking into new, inspiring directions. This challenge causes them to look within and tap into higher values and ideals that inspire them to be passionate about living their best lives. As coaches, we encourage and gently urge them to experiment with new ways of thinking and acting.

3. *Generative competence.* Clients recognize and track their changes in order to acknowledge the meaningful contributions they are making to their lives and to see the positive results of their efforts. They need to experience a sense of

progress so they can be inspired by their best efforts. Coaches can play a key role in providing positive feedback, support, and affirmation to their clients and in helping them see how their efforts are contributing toward their desired future. This in turn helps engender positive feelings of hope and empowerment—a positive reinforcing cycle.

These are wonderful skills for clients to develop as they begin shifting their reliance on external support (for example, their coach) to self-reliance and gaining a sense of empowerment in knowing how to sustain their new actions, behaviors, and practices rather than experiencing them as happening only in relation to the coaching process.

Máirín was a client who incorporated these three competencies in the course of her coaching engagement. She ended in Destiny with the ability to affirm her own strengths, stretch and move into inspiring directions, and develop systems for tracking the progress of her positive changes. She incorporated into her daily life some strategies to build these competencies.

For a time, Máirín struggled with learning how to set boundaries around her relationships at work and with her family. Then she came up with the metaphor of fences. Almost immediately, she was able to set in place a series of multiple fences around herself that were invisible until they were triggered. With this strategy, she felt safe. If she sensed danger or anger, her fences came up out of the "ground" to protect her. They went as high as she needed them to, and she could see through them. They were flexible and were illuminated at night. She described herself before she had the fences as feeling battered or blown around by the energy and emotion of others. The fences gave her choices.

She also liked the metaphor of a kaleidoscope. She found that if she just shifted her focus slightly to the positive when dealing with challenging people or situations, she could often see things differently and feel more empowered. Máirín shared that one of the most significant changes she made in taking care of herself was to do reality checks when she didn't feel positive about herself or the situation she was in. The kaleidoscope image and the reality checks were creative ways Máirín used to connect with self, check her perceptions, and ultimately feel more confident about herself and the world around her.

Supporting the Client in Holding Faith When the Going Gets Tough

Sometimes change happens quickly, especially when a client has been particularly in tune with the energy of this positive method. *Once Diane began to focus on bringing more balance into her professional life, she saw that she had two challenges. First, a lack of administrative support meant that she needed both to sell and to support her sales to customers. Second, the owners of her company had their own squabbles, and it took a lot of Diane's energy to remain out of their fray. Almost as soon as she and her coach were able to define these elements, a former colleague offered her a new position in which both quality administrative support and more nurturing relationships were present. These changes happened quickly, allowing Diane to move toward her larger dream.*

But creating a dream can sometimes take longer. A big dream like Máirín's (to become her own person) affects many facets of an individual's life and only materializes over time. Dreams can also be delayed because of unexpected life circumstances, as in Debra's case, when she had to postpone her search for a dream job as she strove to find immediate work to support her family. None of us can know what turns our lives will take.

These turns can discourage clients. They need their coach to believe in them and in their dream as they re-center themselves and reclaim their dream. Susanna talked about this in a Coaching Prep Form:

"I learned that I am not immune to setbacks because I have been in the midst of one. I know that I can move beyond it, but it has been a difficult time. I have had a series of unproductive days at work, which frustrates me. It helped to have a long weekend off; part of the issue was being fatigued and needing a change of scene. I have also been dis-

tracted with some health concerns. I would like to get back into the
rhythm I had developed earlier and which I have found difficult to
reclaim. I am also still developing a vision of what professional happi-
ness looks like for me."

The coach plays a significant part in this stage by holding faith
with the client that with perseverance and willingness the dream
will come to be. "Momentum for change requires large amounts of
both *positive affect* and *social bonding*—things like hope, inspiration,
and sheer joy in creating with one another."[5] When coach and
client are connected as partners in the positive pursuit of a dream
and when they both retain positive attitudes and act toward the
desired change, the change will happen. This support is especially
needed when life presents our clients with inevitable challenges.

Alan, for example, hit some challenges while moving toward his
dream. As he continued building his consulting practice, he found that
new clients came in irregularly and that he could not control when this
would happen. He had to hold faith that by persevering and focusing on
the marketing endeavors he and his coach had identified, he would make
the necessary connections with future clients. He perceived himself as
having the skills and flexibility to face renewed challenges and as being an
effective actor on his own behalf. The support of his coach helped him
stay focused, keep commitments, and take decisive action.

Saying *Namaste* When Coaching Comes to a Close

In Sanskrit, *namas* means "a bow, obeisance, reverential salutation,
adoration." It comes from the root *nam*, which carries the meanings
of bending, bowing, humbly submitting, and becoming silent. *Te*
means "to you." Thus, *namaste* means "a bow to you" or "I bow to
you." Some say, "The light in me bows to the light in you." There
comes a time in any coaching relationship when it is time to say
namaste to our client. We as coaches bow to them in salutation and
are honored for having been part of their life's journey.

The coaching relationship has transitioned into Destiny when
the client begins to talk about her dream in the present tense and

is regularly engaged in activities that increase confidence in achieving the entire dream. There is a balance between readiness (our
client's readiness to strike out on her own), hesitancy (some sadness
and hesitation to end the relationship), and completion (both the
coach's and the client's sense that they are done with their work
together). Ending the coaching engagement then requires an intu-
itive and delicate touch.

Some clients have confidence and feel sufficiently sure of themselves to end the coaching relationship before their dream is fully realized. They believe they have the focus and skills to move forward on
their own. As coaches, we are fortunate when these clients communicate their continuing achievements even after our formal relationship has ended. Kathy informed her coach of her accomplishments in
qualifying for a company award and being recognized at the annual
meeting—breakthrough experiences in moving toward her dream of
leadership within the company. Rita's coach spoke to her months after
her coaching engagement ended and found her working within the
same company rebuilding the reputation she and her bosses had feared
was permanently damaged. She had also found more time to be with
her children and had joined the parents' board of their school.

Other clients are more hesitant to end the relationship. This is
especially true when organizations dictate the length of a coaching
engagement. Not surprisingly, this can be particularly difficult for
clients who can clearly see what they've achieved with the support
of their coach, but do not feel quite ready to strike out on their own.
These cases require that the coach help the client realize that with
some preparedness, he has the skills and resources to continue on
his own.

*Susanna's coaching ended because she attained the picture of success
she, her boss, and coach had described at the beginning of the engagement, but she felt that she still would have liked more time to master some
practices. As she readied to conclude her coaching sessions, she wrote in
her Coaching Prep Form, "I am worried about ending coaching. I appreciate that we will be in a continuing relationship, but I don't want to*

impose on that. I don't know that I need to continue to have regular sessions; I think the challenge now is for me to continue to practice what we have talked about."

Still other clients have a sense of completion and want to stay in Destiny to savor the realization of their dream. We saw in Chapter Eight how Máirín realized her expansive dream after much effort and support.

When Máirín looked around and saw that her life had become the vision that she had created so long ago, she was in a state of mixed emotions—indescribable joy as well as some fear about whether she might lose it. This is the emotional state of the Destiny Stage—clients are learning to internalize and sustain the reality of their dream. When her coach asked her if she was ready to create her next dream, Máirín responded quite clearly that she wanted to stay right where she was to enjoy and play with the flow she now had to her life. She needed to hold faith for a period of time that this was truly hers. She voiced the importance of taking time to recognize and celebrate what she had achieved. In Máirín's case, there was no need to rush through Destiny to begin the cycle anew. Clients set the pace of their own change.

In the end, of course, coaches do not control when clients feel the coaching relationship has come to an end, but we can watch closely for client readiness. When clients say "I can do this" or "I am different" and we can see the evidence of their ability and growth, the time to end is at hand. The following are things clients might say that serve as clues to readiness:

- I can see that this is possible.

- I am spending more time doing what I want.

- Maybe if we tweaked this a little, it would get me closer to . . .

- I'm feeling pretty confident that I can . . .

- I am really conscious of this now.

- Things just seem to be falling into place.

A Coaching Sequence in the Destiny Stage

There is no prescribed or best way to approach the Destiny Stage. Much has already happened to bring the client to this point, whether the appreciative process moved quickly and sequentially or slowly with many helpful loops back to Discovery or Dream. It is the client who sets the pace and tone. We have, however, identified three steps that usually occur during this final stage:

1. Client and coach identify and celebrate the dream in the present.
2. Client and coach focus on ways to act, expand capabilities, and persevere in realizing the dream.
3. The coach helps prepare the client to move on.

Step One: Client and Coach Identify and Celebrate the Dream in the Present

The coach's main focus in this step is to help the client have a clear picture of where he is going and to celebrate where he is now in manifesting his dream. Celebration is important in this step, as the road to realization for most clients is a challenging one. To maintain feelings of hope and empowerment, it helps to acknowledge accomplishments with lots of positive affect.

Frank started coaching as a talented and determined manager. He had a dream of the kind of company that he wanted to work in, but he had trouble believing in himself and tended to hang back from voicing his opinion and from declaring what he believed was right. Through his coach's consistent reinforcement and focus on his strengths and successes, as well as those of his MBA graduate professors and his boss, Frank began to gain self-confidence. He identified some changes he wanted to see happen in the company, and started working toward them.

Frank wasn't sure at the beginning that he had the full support of the leadership of his company. Then something interesting happened. A ven-

dor, whom he deeply respected, offered him a potential leadership role in another company. Frank, who hadn't really known his own value in the marketplace because he had always worked for one small company, began to believe in himself. He began to believe that his dream of building a company based on vision and principles was possible. Frank's coach helped him celebrate the fact that he might be close to realizing his dream. But in which company would it be?

Step Two: Client and Coach Focus on Ways to Act, Expand Capabilities, and Persevere

The focus in this step is to help the client take action, expand her capabilities, and persevere on her path forward. Together coach and client assess current practices (actions) to make sure that they are productive and energizing and that they lead in the direction of the client's dream. This is a time for building competency and confidence and for determining what more needs to be done.

Frank was learning a lot of management skills in his graduate work and was in the fortunate position of being able to apply them to his job situation. He and his coach worked together to expand on his management knowledge and capabilities and to implement the strategies he found compelling and useful. Although his boss often found Frank's ideas too progressive, Frank persevered in coming to agreement with him in implementing some version of Frank's suggestions. The combination of acquiring broader management skills and greater confidence allowed Frank to stand up for himself more frequently and positively.

Step Three: The Coach Helps Prepare the Client to Move On

In this step, the coach helps the client disengage (say *namaste*) or go around the cycle again. The coach's role in the disengagement is to make sure that the client has the practices and tools he needs to sustain his new direction.

Frank decided in favor of his current employer. The company owners confirmed that they were grooming Frank to take over the company and that they were paying for his MBA education as part of that preparation.

With this decision made, Frank saw his dream with clarity and hope. He had greater confidence and knowledge and more willingness to apply that knowledge. This, combined with his increased tolerance for ambiguity and personality differences, enabled Frank and the current owners to work out an effective transition plan for his new role as leader of the company. Frank ended the coaching engagement prepared to move forward with his newly acquired skills and confidence. He felt that coaching had been critical to maintaining his composure, and he believed he had the capability to carry on by himself. Frank's story about himself is now a very different one—a story filled with his own destiny.

Coaching Tools in the Destiny Stage

The tools of the Destiny Stage are to assist clients in internalizing and sustaining the reality of their dream. As we have stated in the previous stage chapters, these tools are only examples of what you can use as a coach. You may find tools from many other coaching traditions useful as well.

Questions

The primary focus of questions in the Destiny Stage is threefold: to assist the client in thinking about the positive aspects of the present she has created, to celebrate her achievements, and to ensure that she continues to grow into her desired future. There are many questions that can be relevant to ask in this stage. We list a few here to engage your imagination.

- How are you already living your dream?

- Reflect on where we began and where you are today. What's the same or different?

- What makes you proud?

- What do you want to see or do more of to get closer to your dream?

- What still needs conscious attention to be sure that it becomes a natural part of your day?

- What commitments do you make to yourself?

- What has been the most important thing you have learned about yourself?

- How will you continue to care for yourself and receive support for your continued efforts?

- Who has supported you in your journey and deserves your gratitude or recognition?

- How will you continue to foster your own development?

- What compels you now?

- What remains for us to discuss?

Practice

Early research into Appreciative Inquiry and positive imagery included studies of Olympic-level athletes.[6] Cooperrider noted that these athletes not only practiced but also studied their own successes carefully before each performance. Although they were able to assess both poor and exceptional performance, their focus was on envisioning higher performance using their past successes. For any of us to be high performers, we need to do both of these things: we need to practice, and we need to envision ourselves as successful.

In the prior stages, clients experimented to discover their strengths and to try out new behaviors. In Destiny, the focus shifts to making new behaviors habitual through practice. In this final stage of Appreciative Coaching, clients are practicing and examining their achievements with their coach.

Gwynne came to coaching with a desire to be more creative in her life. She worked at a large manufacturing company in a traditional human resources position, which required her to learn complex rules and perform many transactional services for her internal clients. She felt that she could not use her full capabilities and was stifled by the repetitiveness of her job. Feeling the need to give expression to her more creative side, she decided to act on a long-desired dream—to sing. She began lessons and was soon performing, even in front of large groups.

The singing did wonders to revitalize her creativity. During coaching, she realized that she was becoming more extraverted and more confident in her voice and performing skills. The more she practiced singing in her nonwork life, the more singing changed her whole life. Through their conversations, her coach helped Gwynne crystallize what was happening, be more conscious of it, and act on it more explicitly. Through practice, she honed skills in one context so that they became habitual and transferable to her work context. They were becoming a natural part of her. The act and practice of singing were helping her express who she really was. People at work began to notice differences and commented on her growing interpersonal skills. Her job became more challenging and engaging when she was asked to address sensitive issues with clients. In reflection with her coach, Gwynne realized that practicing these skills in a nonthreatening environment helped her integrate the creative and rational parts of herself—something she felt she could not have done in the more restrictive work environment.

Perseverance

Beginning to make personal changes, although not easy, is often exhilarating. Then the going often gets tougher, and people may become frustrated or tired. As coaches, we recognize that periods of slowness or feeling stuck come about, and we must dig into our toolboxes to help clients persevere through these times. It is then that we must remember the principles and act on them so that our clients can benefit. For example, the Positive Principle tells us that emotions amplify. As coaches, we act on this by holding confidence for our clients that they will make it through this period; they feel our confidence even though they may waver. The Anticipatory Principle says that people continually move toward their images of the future. We act on this principle by reminding our clients of the specifics of their dreams and what they have already accomplished in moving toward their desires.

We help our clients hold their attention on their dream and take action each day. Often one setback can send them into a tailspin, so we review their achievements, celebrate with them, and help them find other practices if some are proving not to be fruitful. We inspire them, remind them, and help them persevere. Here are some tools, some of which may already be familiar to you, that we suggest to clients to support them through these periods:

- Putting a physical representation of their dream in a position where they can see it easily and often.

- Selecting a small object that is a representation of the dream and carrying it where they can touch and handle it. It can be a small memento, such as a beautiful stone or a picture.

- Arranging with another person, a friend or mentor, to call occasionally to ask how they are doing and to remind them of their dream.

- Finding ways to center each day and be inspired to act.

- Asking themselves if they are willing to really "be in the present" and take some action in their benefit.

- Using their observing selves to be aware of the opportunities that present themselves and to take action.

- Deciding on a particular action when feeling ambivalent.

- Focusing on blessings and expressing gratitude when life seems to hit a rough patch.

Celebration

Celebration is the act of savoring, appreciating, and rejoicing. Although clients may enjoy helping others celebrate, they often neglect to do it for themselves and just move on to the next moment of their lives. They forget to appreciate where they are and what they have accomplished. Just as we paid great attention to the positive in our clients' lives in Discovery, we give the same attention in Destiny. We help them find ways to bring celebration into their lives as they move forward and disengage with us. Here are some ideas that we suggest to clients:

- Consider acts of celebration that are meaningful to them: How do they like to celebrate? What feels good?

- Share good feelings by identifying friends or colleagues to create a "celebration support group."

- Write about their accomplishments or feelings in a journal or in letters to themselves.

- Find quiet moments to stop and savor their accomplishments, good situation, or positive feeling.

Finally, we celebrate with our clients that it is time to end the coaching relationship. As a former coach of our own once said, "We are always in relationship." We are happy to have our clients continue to share their stories with us as they move on in life.

Summary

The Destiny Stage is about helping clients internalize and live the reality of their dream. It is about sustaining what they have achieved. The focus of the coach in this stage is on four activities: helping the client recognize and celebrate his dream, guiding him in ways to expand his capacity, holding faith with him, and, when the time comes, saying *namaste*.

We presented three steps for coaches to focus on in the Destiny Stage. In the first step, the coach helps the client identify and celebrate those aspects of her dream she is already living in the present. In the second step, the coach encourages the client to take action, expand her capabilities, and persevere on her path forward. And in the third step, the coach helps prepare the client to move on. At this point the client may disengage or may decide to embrace a larger dream, thereby entering another Appreciative Coaching cycle.

This chapter also offered some valuable tools we use in this stage: asking Destiny questions, helping clients identify what they need to practice, supporting clients in persevering toward their dream, and celebrating when they arrive.

In the next chapter, we suggest ways in which you may want to experiment with Appreciative Coaching. We offer several tools for integrating aspects of our method into an existing or new coaching practice or for beginning to adopt Appreciative Coaching as your own primary method.

10

Stepping into Appreciative Coaching

We must not sit down and wait for miracles. Up, and be going!
John Eliot (1604–1690), British Puritan missionary

Incorporating Appreciative Coaching into our personal and professional lives has been a stimulating, challenging, and rewarding experience. We thought it might be helpful to share some of the steps we followed in this process for those of you interested in weaving Appreciative Coaching into your own coaching practices. We suggest a number of key ways that you can use Appreciative Coaching in the field of coaching:

- Embracing it as the primary coaching model and approach in a coaching practice

- Employing it as an additional tool in an established coaching practice

- Applying selectively such elements as appreciative language, questions, and tools to enhance other coaching methods

- Training managers and supervisors in appreciative coaching skills

- Presenting the underlying theory, principles, and stages of Appreciative Coaching in an educational or training context

Our intention is to make the theory, practice, and examples presented in our book helpful and thought-provoking, no matter what the level of the coach—from those in training to master-level practitioners. From our research and experience with Appreciative Coaching, we have found that the approach works effectively in a range of coaching situations or applications: executive coaching, organizational coaching, small business coaching, performance coaching, and life coaching. We have also provided skill training to some clients in applying the Appreciative Coaching approach as managers or as coaches.

In this chapter, we highlight four key steps we experienced as we incorporated Appreciative Coaching into our own practices: addressing worldview, using appreciative language, understanding what clients bring, and becoming familiar with the stages and principles. We also include some specific tools that were helpful to us in bringing the appreciative approach into our work. We offer these as information to help you decide whether and how to incorporate Appreciate Coaching into your own professional practices.

Addressing Worldview

Early on, we found ourselves discussing the importance of clarifying our own worldview and its alignment with Appreciative Coaching as a way to become more comfortable with the approach. The term *worldview* comes from the German *Weltanschauung*, meaning a view or perspective on the world or universe that describes one's total outlook, including beliefs and assumptions about reality, human nature, and the meaning and nature of life itself. In the largest sense, we all have an interpretative lens or filter we use to understand our reality and existence, and this lens develops over time.[1]

Worldview is now understood by researchers as an essential component of human nature, a psychological construct that affects behavior and attitudes.[2] Koltko-Rivera offers a model of worldview that captures for us the significance and impact that this concept has on Appreciative Coaching.[3] This model represents an integrated theory of the psychology of worldviews that is founded on the belief that a person's behavior is consistent with her worldview. Further, an individual's experiences with others help shape the self and therefore the worldview. This is consistent with the social constructionist view that "existence itself is uninterpretable without a worldview."[4]

Koltko-Rivera's model supports the recent focus on Positive Psychology. He identifies numerous areas where worldview could have a significant impact: happiness, positive emotions, selection of life goals, development of human strengths, maintaining well-being, and resilience in times of crisis.[5] By the time a person reaches adulthood, the accumulation of beliefs has merged into a worldview that remains fairly constant unless a crisis or trauma happens to cause a disruption.[6]

We believe that periods of self-discovery and insight can illuminate a person's worldview, which in turn increases her ability to cope with complexity and change in her life. We believe that coaches benefit from examining their worldviews so that they practice from a conscious and definable framework they can express to clients. Appreciative Coaching implies a particular worldview based on the acceptance of the theories of social constructionism, positive methods, and a holistic view of time.

Suggested Tools

Worldviews encompass a person's beliefs and values. There are three lenses for viewing beliefs.[7] Beliefs can be existential—that is, descriptive of what someone perceives to be fundamentally true about the world (God exists to protect me; free will exists; scientific research establishes the truth). Beliefs can be evaluative—that is, judgments about what is good or bad (humans are basically good; people are inherently selfish). Beliefs can be prescriptive or proscriptive—that is, they express a preferred means or ends (I follow the Golden Rule; we live in the moment). Values function like prescriptive or proscriptive beliefs, guiding a person in his actions and behaviors. A person's worldview includes all these kinds of beliefs.

We've included some questions here that may help you bring your own worldview to light. These are also appropriate and salutary questions to ask clients during the Discovery Stage, as they help reveal how clients see themselves in the world.

- What are your three most important values?

- Describe your beliefs about what motivates people (for example, people are basically self-serving, people seek relationships and cooperation).

- What do you not believe?

- How do you experience your environment? (Is the world a friendly place? A jungle? A mystery? A garden of delight?)

- In what ways has your experience and your education changed your view of the world?

- When you find yourself making a difficult decision, which beliefs are in opposition (for example, beliefs about justice and mercy or truth and loyalty)?

- Would you say that your view of life or the world is the same or similar to that of your parents? If not, what has made your view different?

- How do your beliefs affect your relationship with clients and how you coach?

Responses to these questions can help you more closely define your worldview and thereby your level of comfort with an appreciative approach. In Chapter Two, we highlighted two additional assessments that are available online for free or at little cost: the Gallup Organization's StrengthsFinder (www.strengthsfinder.com) and Martin Seligman's Signature Strengths Questionnaire (www.authentichappiness.sas.upenn.edu). These assessments help clarify your strengths. One suggestion is to find a colleague or friend, review the results together, and then debrief the experience by affirming each other. Defining your strengths may be a part of clarifying your own worldview.

Using Appreciative Language

Language matters, especially in coaching. It is the primary tool of our profession and a powerful construct with which to work. As a method grounded in social constructionism—the notion that people create their relationships and their world through language and action—Appreciative Coaching makes extensive use of significantly positive language to generate positive feelings, actions, and outcomes.

We adapted the five principles and four stages of Appreciative Inquiry into our Appreciative Coaching process so that we and our clients might benefit from its forward-reaching and creative orientation. The stages and principles have developed over many years of successful group and organizational change processes using positive and envisioning language. In our coaching approach, we have consistently attempted to select and use language that adheres to this positive foundation. Initially, however, we each went through a period of transition while getting comfortable with the appreciative language, especially the four core questions. At first, it seemed contrived or naive to use appreciative language when our clients wanted to talk about their problems. And why shouldn't we ask questions about clients' problems?

Our coaching research protocol, however, bound us to the use of appreciative questions and to reflection on our clients' and our own reactions to the questions. Through this experimental phase, we each discovered the deep value of following an appreciative line of inquiry. We began to make distinctions between some of the words we used, such as *topic, picture of success, goal, dream, experimentation, actions*, and *practice*, as we've discussed in previous chapters. We found that because of their cultural and business connotation, some words—such as *goals, action plans, skill gaps*, and *status quo*—led more easily to a problem-solving orientation with clients. Other words—*affirmation, images, dreams*, and *potential*—led to a generative orientation with clients. Some of our clients surprised us with their metaphorical and poetic language. In every case, the client responded positively to the continued use of appreciative language, which in turn encouraged us to use more positive, generative language. We found ourselves in a positive self-reinforcing cycle with appreciative language.

We expect that this evolution of learning may happen for you as well. Each of us has now developed our own style and level of comfort with appreciative language, and we encourage you to undertake your own experiments. For example, we found that audiotaping sessions with clients and attending to the words we used most frequently were immensely helpful. How many words were positive, neutral, or problem-oriented? Which words led clients to a positive resolution or positive affect? Which ones left them dissatisfied or restless? We learned to become more appreciative by gradually increasing the number of positive words we used, substituting neutral or problem-oriented language with more inspirational and affirming words.

At first we weren't sure how our clients would respond to a predominance of appreciative or positive language. For most clients, their first coaching encounter with appreciative language involved responding to the four core questions in the first session.

As coaches, we all went through an adjustment phase in becoming comfortable with using those questions. We wondered how our coaching clients would react to the query, "What gives life to you now?" Would they know what we meant by it? Would we sound unprofessional? Would they take us seriously as coaches?

We found we had to fight our own anxiety about our clients' silence when asked such profound questions. Some found it bewildering or difficult to respond to these questions. But we never experienced a client's refusing to answer or being frustrated or angry about the questions. Most clients, once they started speaking about what gave them life and what they most valued, were encouraged by our affirmation and their own positive feelings and began to settle into the conversation and enjoy the exchange.

For some of our clients, this interchange was an eye-opening, exhilarating experience in which they gained unexpected awareness. We heard such comments as these:

- I felt so much energy in thinking about these questions.

- It has been a long time since someone asked me to think about my peak experiences.

- This made me remember times when I felt really proud of myself and what I did.

- This made me realize what I want more of right now.

- I had the luxury of reflection. I don't remember what I like to do—if given an afternoon I wouldn't know what to do. Makes me think about the meaning of life.

Suggested Tools

We arrived at a number of ways to help us become more familiar and comfortable with the questions:

- We answered the questions ourselves or found a partner to ask us the questions so we could truly understand them from our perspective.

- We took time after coaching sessions to write down and reflect on our responses and those of our clients.

- We experimented with possible variants to the questions and allowed the variants to reflect whatever meaning was appropriate to the clients. Some clients responded better to a more lighthearted approach, such as, "What energizes you?" Other clients preferred a deep, soul-searching perspective, such as, "What gives you joy? What is most important to you in life?" We learned to trust that each translation was appropriate and capable of drawing out memories and thoughts about the clients' life that had meaning for them.

- We learned to anticipate a variety of client responses; some people need time to ponder the deep meaning of the questions, some have immediate answers, and others fall in between.

Understanding What Clients Bring

As we discussed in Chapter Five, clients tend to present us with inspiring opportunities to learn and develop. We told the story of Laura, whose response to Appreciative Coaching looked different when compared to the other two coaching research clients. Our experience with Laura caused us to reflect on the assumptions we held about what an Appreciative Coaching client looked like and which of them would find value in our approach. We realized that clients come to us with varying levels of experience and facility in the areas of self-analysis and self-discovery and with different styles of speaking to describe and understand themselves and to construct a positive outlook.

On the one hand, we might venture to say that the greater the client's level of experience and facility in these areas, the more responsive and profound the resonance with Appreciative Coaching will be for that client. On the other hand, it is not entirely clear in all instances how we are to judge clients' reactions. For example, Laura rated the coaching experience very high, and she accomplished most of the priorities she set for herself, although her coach was not sure how much Laura enjoyed the process as it was occurring. We prefer not to speculate about which kinds of clients may be better suited to this method. Instead, we take the view that most clients will respond to a positive method and approach that supports them in learning to be agents of their own actions and attitudes. However, we recognize that there are coaching situations in which the appreciative approach may not be the best or only choice—for example, with clients needing immediate resolution to a problem (although most coaches would probably inquire into the client's ideal solution), with situations involving gap analysis or benchmarking, or with clients seeking specific skill deficit training.

Suggested Tools

Here are some ways in which we prepare and learn about prospective or new clients' level of experience and facility with self-discovery:

- We ask clients to complete a Client Information Form (see Appendix B) that uses appreciative language. It asks what kinds of experience and background they have with self-reflection, self-development, and affirmation.

- We deepen our understanding of our clients' background (work, family situation, education, and health) in the first coaching session.

- We make inquiries about the clients' participation in adult helping relationships, such as mentoring, counseling, or support groups. Those who have not participated in such relationships may need extra time and experience to establish a trusting, positive partnership.

- We focus on topics using positive or at least neutral language, continue to present a positive attitude as a coach, and use miracle questions, all of which tend to engage clients in their own positive process.

Becoming Familiar with Appreciative Coaching Stages and Principles

The five principles and the four stages make up the core of the Appreciative Coaching approach. In our experience, the four stages are the easiest to understand, as they can be visually represented and serve as a ready framework for how the process moves in a clockwise (but not always sequential) manner. Taking a client through all four stages is obviously the only and best way to experience the magic of the whole process. In some cases, coaches might invite a colleague to try out the approach together—learning from one another.

We find the Discovery Stage is the easiest to grasp—it's the beginning stage, and there are concrete questions that help guide the coach in the process. It is a logical place to begin experimenting with the Appreciative Coaching approach, starting with the four core appreciative questions. Coaches can begin practicing by first asking themselves the core questions to discover their own strengths and past successes. Once they obtain a feel for the approach, they might ask the questions of family members, friends, and colleagues. At the same time, they can experiment, using the core questions with new coaching clients or existing clients.

A simple, effective way to become more familiar with any of the four stages is to begin using some of the appreciative and positive questions we have identified for that stage. In addition, you can use the core questions from the Discovery Stage again in the Dream Stage as catalysts for helping clients access their desires and wants, and you can use them in the Destiny Stage as a form of exit strategy to pique clients' interest in what comes next.

As we stated in Chapter Three, the appreciative principles shape the theory and form the foundation of Appreciative Coaching. Like the warp threads of a handmade rug, they are philosophically strong and resilient enough to form the base on which the Appreciative Coaching stages can be woven. One way of understanding the power and significance of the principles is to reflect on the coaching conversation and identify examples of the principles in action. In Chapters Three and Four, we provided suggestions for how to use the principles with clients. Here are some ways to think about the principles during coaching conversations:

- *Constructionist Principle:* During sessions, watch for statements about clients' self-knowledge and for the way they construct their view of their lives, jobs, and families. Invite clients to see themselves in a more holistic manner—instead of focusing only on their failings, they can also recognize their special abilities and gifts.

- *Positive Principle:* Focus on introducing or amplifying positive affect around clients' strengths and accomplishments. "Pivot" clients during sessions by rephrasing problem language into something more positive.

- *Poetic Principle:* Attend to what stories clients tell about themselves. Take advantage of situations to help clients rewrite parts of their stories by seeing themselves in a new light, recognizing new opportunities, or turning liabilities into strengths.

- *Simultaneity Principle:* Remember that inquiry is change and that the "right" questions can help clients see their challenge or situation in a new light. Track the links between positive inquiry and where it leads clients.

- *Anticipatory Principle:* You can be instrumental in helping clients create positive images for themselves through affirmations and visualizations. It is innately human for people to anticipate their future.

Suggested Tools

Reflection and observation were the most effective ways we found to link the theory to the practice of Appreciative Coaching. They helped us examine our own assumptions and see where our experiences contradicted those assumptions; they enabled us to change our coaching behaviors to match our learnings. We recorded our experiences, feelings, and reactions as well as basic facts and outcomes of our coaching conversations. We recommend using a journal, index cards, a small tape recorder, or a mind map.[8] You can use whatever journaling tool makes sense and is comfortable. It could be as simple as quickly typing up reflections and observations on a computer right after each session. We found it helpful to reflect about the same things (categories) each time so we could detect any patterns. Following is a list of items you could choose from:

- Session date

- Brief synopsis of session

- What was my goal for the session?

- What did my client say was most important to accomplish in the session?

- What stage (Discover, Dream, Design, Destiny) were we in? What evidence demonstrated this?

- What evidence did I see of an Appreciative Coaching principle (Constructionist, Simultaneity, Poetic, Anticipatory, Positive)? Which one and how?

- In what ways did I use my client's existing successes and strengths in codesigning a desired future?

- To what degree was the client's language positive?

- To what degree were my questions and responses couched in positive language?

- Is the client experimenting? How?

- What were my feelings during the session?

- How did I feel physically during the session?

- How did the session flow?

- What triggers (words or phrases that spark a strong emotional reaction) did I notice?

- What was the client's affect (voice, tone, pace, enthusiasm, deadpan) at the outset and conclusion of the session?

- How hard did I have to work?

- What did I learn during the session or as a result of the session?

Answering three to five of these questions over a number of coaching sessions is an effective way to begin to get a sense of what the appreciative approach is all about. Although it took some discipline to write in our journals after each session, we found the reflection well worth the effort. By the end of a coaching engagement, we were able to see how and in what ways our learnings deepened.

Summary

This chapter offered four key ways to begin introducing an appreciative perspective into new or existing coaching practices: addressing worldview, using appreciative language, understanding what clients bring, and becoming familiar with the appreciative stages and principles. We also included some tools that we found helpful. On our own paths of incorporating Discovery, Dream, Design, and

Destiny into our coaching businesses, we relied heavily on reflection, observation, experimentation, and practice. We were continually engaged in these important activities, and we expect that you will be as well. The other activity that was very helpful to us was sharing and discussing our experiences and learnings with one another. We encourage you to add this dimension as well.

A Final Word

All coaches want their clients to succeed, and they help them achieve success using whatever approach seems most effective. We also think that, beyond success, flourishing is important to our clients, to the country, and to the world. If we as coaches find ways to help people flourish, we will have done our jobs well. If we can help clients accept themselves as fully capable and autonomous agents in making choices, if we can help them master their environments, have positive relations with those around them, and pursue a purpose about which they feel passionate, we have contributed to a more empowered and effective human family.[9]

A Glossary of Terms

As with all philosophies, there are certain terms that come to define their uniqueness. This section describes those terms most frequently used in Appreciative Coaching.

The Five Appreciative Principles

The five principles form the foundation on which Appreciative Coaching is built.

Constructionist Principle

The Constructionist Principle posits that knowing and becoming are interwoven. Who a person is now and how she became who she is now are strong predictors of who she can and will become. A person's future is an extension of what she knows and doesn't know.

Examples of the Constructionist Principle in Action

- Questions or discussion that help the client see his past successes and abilities

- Initiating questions that lay a foundation for a possible future

- Application of past successes and abilities to new areas

Positive Principle

Positive attitudes, actions, and connections influence long-term change. The Positive Principle suggests that when both the coach and the client are connected in the positive pursuit of a dream, and when they both retain (mostly) positive attitudes and act toward the desired change, the change will happen positively.

Examples of the Positive Principle in Action

- Positive bonding between the coach and client

- Positive conversation in which the coach and client build on each other's ideas

- Demonstration of positive affect by either the coach or client (for example, expressions of hope, joy, inspiration)

Simultaneity Principle

According to the Simultaneity Principle, inquiry and change happen in the same moment. To put it another way, the future happens in and as a result of the present. The seeds of change are sown by the very first questions coaches ask and create foundations for what our clients discover. These discoveries become foundations for dreaming and for designing destinies.

Examples of the Simultaneity Principle in Action

- Questioning by the coach that prompts the client to think in a new way

- Discussion by coach or client of what may be possible

- Change in language by the client from negative or neutral to positive

Poetic Principle

The Poetic Principle suggests that an individual's story can be rewritten to better fit how the person sees herself in the present or future. Any number of new realities can flow from a reinterpretation of one's life story, just as there are any number of potential interpretations of a poem. A person's life story can be reframed, reimagined, and refocused toward more hopeful and joyful action.

Examples of the Poetic Principle in Action

- Reframing of a neutral or negative story by the coach, which helps the client see new possibilities

- Moments of creativity when the client discovers he has choices

- Joy in the client for having made positive changes or achieved positive outcomes in his life

Anticipatory Principle

The Anticipatory Principle states that a particular dream of the future can guide current behavior in the direction of that future. Focusing the client on her particular vision or dream enables clearer action in the present toward that vision.

Examples of the Anticipatory Principle in Action

- A client's imagining what the future might be like

- A coach's suggesting actions toward a future dream

- A client's suggesting or reporting actions toward his dream

The Four Appreciative Stages

These four stages define the pathway through an Appreciative Coaching process.

Discovery Stage

Discovery is the first stage of Appreciative Coaching and sets the tone for the process. It is about truly appreciating what gives life to our clients. The purpose of the Discovery Stage is to help clients focus on an appreciative view of themselves and the topic or situation they bring to the coaching relationship.

Coach's Focus in the Discovery Stage

- Establishing a positive connection between coach and client

- Leading the client to a more empowering perspective

- Affirming a sense of the possible

- Cultivating and supporting the client's belief in a positive future

Dream Stage

The purpose of the Dream Stage is to support our clients in articulating a meaningful picture of the future—a picture that is of their own choosing. We encourage them to stretch beyond the limits of a comfortable self-image so that they create a vision powerful enough to give them the inspiration and direction to actualize a true dream.

Coach's Focus in the Dream Stage

- Encouraging the client to create images of possibilities

- Inviting the client to give voice to her preferred future

- Affirming the client's dream

Design Stage

The Design Stage is about helping clients direct their attention and take action so that they become the designers of the future they most desire. The purpose of this stage is to provide a structure and foundation for clients to proactively attain their dream.

Coach's Focus in the Design Stage

- Assisting the client in bringing the dream into focus

- Affirming the reality of the dream

- Supporting mindful choices and actions

Destiny Stage

People's lives and destinies are always in the process of creation. The Destiny Stage is not about endings or even beginnings; it is about living one's life fully and well. The purpose of this stage is for clients to internalize and live the reality of their dream.

Coach's Focus in the Destiny Stage

- Helping the client recognize his dreams in the present

- Enabling the client to expand her capacity to create her dream

- Supporting the client in holding faith when the going gets tough

- Saying *namaste* when coaching comes to a close

Appendix A

Our Research Methodology

Appreciative Coaching as presented in this book is based on the prior work of many researchers and practitioners. It is also based on our own experiences with clients and on our learnings from a qualitative research project. This research was conducted in two phases. Its methodology is summarized here.

Overall Research Question

Would the principles and practices of the Appreciative Inquiry approach used in organization development make a successful coaching model?

Research Time Line

Phase I: September 2004 to February 2005
Phase II: March 2005 to November 2005

Research Protocol for Phase I

Each researcher

- Worked with three clients for nine sessions each

- Recorded observations after each coaching session, following a protocol

- Collected evaluations from all clients midway through coaching and at the end

Research Protocol for Phase II

Each researcher:

- Worked with one client for nine sessions each

- Tape-recorded the conversations

- Recorded observations after each coaching session, following a protocol

- Collected evaluations from all clients midway through coaching and at the end

Following the coaching sessions in phase II,

- The tape-recorded conversations were transcribed.

- Three external coders, following a prepared protocol, each reviewed a transcript to indicate where he or she saw evidence of Appreciative Coaching stages and principles.

Other Elements of the Research Protocol

In both phases, we incorporated the following elements:

- Clients were asked to complete the Client Information Form.

- Each coach asked the four core appreciative questions in the first coaching session.

- We used the Appreciative Coaching stages and principles to the best of our ability while coaching.

- We used a prepared form for our observations and reflections after each coaching session. This form included such topics as the use of language and positive questions, experimentation, leveraging of strengths and successes, and indicators of the stages and principles.

- Client feedback also followed a prepared form and was requested at midpoint and at the completion of coaching.

Presentation of Research

We have presented our research to the coaching community at three ICF Coaching Research Symposiums both in the United States and in Europe. We also presented to our academic colleagues at the Fielding Graduate University. These colleagues recommended the protocol that became our second phase of research. We are grateful to all our colleagues for their enthusiasm and suggestions. The final results, of course, are incorporated into this book.

Appendix B

Client Information Form

Please fill out this form and return to your coach.

Name _____ Home phone _____

Address_____ Work phone _____

City _____ Work extension _____

State/Province _____ Mobile phone _____

Postal code _____ E-mail _____

Country _____ 2nd e-mail _____

Occupation _____ Title _____

Company _____ Marital status/children _____

Education _____

Certificates, workshops, etc. _____

How did you hear about me? _____

Your History

Describe your three greatest accomplishments to date.

What made these accomplishments stand out for you?

What have you incorporated into your current actions from your past accomplishments?

How could you use what you've learned from these accomplishments to assist you in making future changes?

What major transitions have you had in the past two years? (For example, new assignment, new residence, new relationship, etc.)

If you worked with a coach before or a similar one-on-one adult relationship (for example, tennis coach, piano teacher, therapist), what worked well for you?

If you have worked with a coach, and you are not currently, how did that relationship end?

Your Life

Who are or have been your major role models?

What attributes of these role models do you admire and want to emulate?

What are the five most positive things in your life?

What are five things you would like to change in your life that would make it even more satisfying, effective, and joyful? (Examples include relationships, information, environment, job.)

Who are the key supportive people in your life, and what do they provide for you?

On a scale of 1 to 10 (1 being least effective and 10 being most effective), rate the quality of your life. ____ By what criteria did you rate yourself?

What percentage of the life you are leading is actually YOUR life?

Your Self Today

List five adjectives that describe you at your best.

What prevents you from being at your best?

What energizes you?

What saps your energy?

What are you learning and accepting about yourself at present?

In what ways do you currently spend time, that if you were to spend it differently, would yield greater happiness and achievement?

What do you consume now, that if you didn't, would allow you to be healthier? (For example, alcohol, caffeine, sugar.)

Could therapy effectively resolve some issue in your life now?

Your Potential

What is your personal and/or professional vision?

What would you like to contribute to the world?

What are you most wanting to achieve in the next three years?

What are you most wanting to achieve in the next six months?

How ready are you to go for it?

Use the boxes below as thought starters for the goals above.

Family/home	Relationships
Financial situation	Leisure time
Career or business	Self-care
Personal character	Learning

Making It Happen

Why have you hired me?

What are three immediate changes you can make to get you off to a good start in our coaching?

How can I help you to be more effective in working toward your goals?

Here are ways coaching clients work with me. Which of these appeal to you? (Select as many as apply.)

☐ Brainstorming strategies together

☐ Support, encouragement, and validation

☐ Insight into who you are and your potential

☐ Painting a vision of what you can become or accomplish

☐ Exploring possibilities and building on past success

☐ Accountability; checking up on goals

☐ Suggesting or designing action steps that lead to greater effectiveness and joy

What approaches to change have you found less effective for you?

What responsibility do you have for ensuring that our relationship works well?

How will you know that your coaching experience has been effective?

Thank you for filling out the form.

Appendix C

Coaching Prep Form

The purpose of this form is to help you reflect on the time since our last coaching meeting and to help us focus our coaching conversation. Please fill out the form by placing your responses in the boxes. Please complete the form in advance of our next coaching meeting and e-mail to your coach the evening before our scheduled time.

Name	
Date of Next Call	
Accomplished or Learned	
Remains to Be Accomplished	
High Points	
Grateful for	
Other Comments	

Notes

Introduction

1. Please see Appendix A for a summary of our research project.
2. Berger & Luckmann, 1966.
3. Gallwey, 1974.

Chapter One

1. The concept of taking on 100 percent responsibility, no more or less, comes from Caldwell (1996). Caldwell says that in any situation, individuals need to take on the responsibility that is theirs—100 percent. Taking on less responsibility creates guilt, and taking on more creates a burden. Alan is speaking to his desire to take on all the responsibility that is his, but no more.
2. Mihaly Csikszentmihalyi, a professor of psychology at the University of Chicago, is best known for his seminal work, *Flow: The Psychology of Optimal Experience* (1990).
3. Rilke, 1987.
4. Watkins & Mohr, 2001.

Chapter Two

1. Wheatley, 1992.
2. Watkins & Mohr, 2001.
3. Cooperrider & Srivastva, 1987, p. 15.

4. Berger & Luckmann, 1966.

5. Seligman & Csikszentmihalyi, 2000.

6. Cooperrider, 1990, p. 92.

7. Watkins & Mohr, 2001; Whitney & Trosten-Bloom, 2003.

8. Watkins & Mohr, 2001.

9. Cooperrider, 1986; Cooperrider & Srivastva, 1987.

10. Cooperrider, 1990.

11. Cooperrider, Whitney, & Stavros, 2003.

12. Cooperrider et al., 2003, p. 4.

13. Hammond, 1998.

14. Watkins & Mohr, 2001, p. xxxi.

15. Cameron, Dutton, & Quinn, 2003.

16. Luthans & Avolio, 2003.

17. Wrzesniewski, 2003.

18. Dutton, 2003.

19. Worline & Quinn, 2003.

20. Seligman & Csikszentmihalyi, 2000.

21. Seligman & Csikszentmihalyi, 2000, p. 13.

22. Seligman & Csikszentmihalyi, 2000, p. 7.

23. Seligman found that each of us displays or uses three to five of the twenty-four signature strengths as primary strengths. He makes his VIA Signature Strengths Survey available on his Web site for any-one wishing to deepen her exploration of her strengths. See www.authentichappiness.sas.upenn.edu.

24. This belief closely mirrors the Poetic Principle of Appreciative Inquiry.

25. Diener & Seligman, 2004.

26. Cited in Seligman, 2002.

27. Csikszentmihalyi, 1990.

28. Goleman, 1995.

29. Timothy Wilson is a social psychologist from the University of Virginia, George Loewenstein an economist from Carnegie-Mellon, Daniel Kahneman a psychologist from Princeton and a Nobel laureate in economics, and Daniel Gilbert a psychologist from Harvard.

30. See Gertner, 2003.

31. Wilson, 2002.

32. Weakland, Fisch, Watzlawick, & Bodin, 1974, p. 142.

33. Weakland, Fisch, Watzlawick, & Bodin, 1974.

34. Insoo Kim Berg, "Student's Corner," available from www.brief-therapy.org/insoo_essays.htm.

35. Lethem, 2002.

36. de Shazer et al., 1986, p. 211.

37. Insoo Kim Berg, "Hot Tips," available from www.brief-therapy.org/insoo_essays.htm.

38. Lethem, 2002, p. 190.

39. de Shazer et al., 1986.

40. Insoo Kim Berg, "Hot Tips," available from www.brief-therapy.org/insoo_essays.htm.

41. We wish to acknowledge that Insoo Kim Berg and Peter Szabo have cowritten a book and developed a coaching method, both called *Brief Coaching for Lasting Solutions*, using the core SFBT practices in coaching.

42. Gable & Haidt, 2005.

Chapter Three

1. Watkins & Mohr, 2001.

2. Cooperrider & Whitney, 2001, p. 15.

3. Sociologists Berger and Luckmann initially introduced this view in their work *Social Construction of Reality* (1966). More recently, such AI theorists as Cooperrider, Srivastva, and Whitney have drawn heavily on the work of Kenneth Gergen, who believed that social actions gain their meaning from a community of agreement. Recognition and

acceptance of this view legitimize much of the current research and practice in this area and have resulted in much innovation and creativity in organizational change.

4. Chaffee, 2004.

5. Mohr, 2004.

6. The language examples in Table 3.1 and those in the coming chapters were identified from our coaching research.

7. Quinn & Quinn (2002), as cited in Roberts, Dutton, Spreitzer, Heaphy, & Quinn, 2005, p. 715.

8. As cited in Fredrickson, 1998.

9. Fredrickson, 1998.

10. Seligman, 2002.

11. Cooperrider & Srivastva, 1987.

12. Seligman, 2002.

13. Fredrickson, 1998.

14. The Positive Principle in Appreciative Inquiry grew out of years of experience in organizations. AI practitioners discovered that in order to build and sustain change, people needed both positive feeling and social bonding (Cooperrider & Whitney, 1999a). When employees were able to share positive emotions—such as hope, excitement, inspiration, caring, camaraderie, a sense of purpose, and just sheer joy in working together on something meaningful—they were able to move more energetically toward a desired change.

Indeed, Cooperrider found that the more positive the questions asked, the more long lasting and successful the change effort. He saw a clear link between positive, life-enhancing inquiry and positive action. He felt that AI practitioners were much more effective the more they were able to learn, admire, be surprised at, and be inspired by the people they were working with. He also found that when individuals reflected on a time when they were valued or appreciated, they experienced a variety of positive emotions (Cooperrider & Sekerka, 2003).

15. Barbara Fredrickson won the Templeton Positive Psychology Prize in 2000 for her theory of the function of positive emotions (Seligman, 2002).

16. Roberts et al., 2005.

17. Hatfield, Cacioppo, & Rapson, 1994.

18. Doherty, 1997.

19. Fredrickson, 2003.

20. Fredrickson, 1998, p. 300.

21. Fredrickson, 1998.

22. Fredrickson, 1998.

23. Fredrickson, 1998.

24. Judge, T. A., & Ilies, R., 2004.

25. Fredrickson, 1998.

26. Seligman, 2002.

27. Cooperrider, 1990.

28. Cooperrider, 1990, p. 99.

29. Cooperrider, 1990.

30. Cooperrider, 1990.

31. Judge, T. A., & Ilies, R., 2004.

32. Roberts et al., 2005, p. 712.

33. Roberts et al., 2005.

34. A jolt or trigger event is defined as a discontinuity in the environment, which causes individuals to try to make sense of it. Jolts can be major (losing a job, birth of a child, a promotion) or minor (receiving new information that serves as a tipping point to change). Jolts are significant because they disrupt the automatic information processing and habitual ways of thinking about the self. They detach people momentarily from their routine thinking and release emotions that can help them change by causing them to move away from the old and to focus energy toward the future.

A jolt can be an "Aha" experience that triggers an immediate need to make sense of the situation or reveals aspects of oneself that previously have been hidden (Roberts et al., 2005).

35. These resources identified by Roberts et al. (2005) are similar to those identified in Fredrickson's positive emotion model (1998).

36. Roberts et al., 2005.

Chapter Four

1. We are indebted to Brent Slife (1993), who researched the role of linear time in psychological explanations and identified alternative views of time in past and current methodologies and approaches.

2. Boltz, 2006.

3. We acknowledge that there are current theories of psychological change and coaching that are not past-oriented. Although we may refer to some, undoubtedly we will omit others. We do not intend this to be a comprehensive study but rather a description of a significant "new" view of time that, if grasped, can have a strong impact on coaches interested in using an appreciative approach.

4. We acknowledge that the study of time is complex and rich with fiery debate among disciplines about its very definition and its multiple manifestations.

5. Newton, 1687/1990.

6. The acceptance of Newton's Absolute Time was supported by the rise of industrialism and its need for scheduling and controlling factory workers and transportation of goods, and by the resulting manufacture of cheap watches. Western societies settled on Newton's linear time as the only interpretation or construction of time.

7. Clancy, 1996.

8. Lewin, 1948.

9. We are indebted to Slife (1993), who described the five characteristics of Newtonian time as they relate to current psychological explanations.

10. In Newtonian time, subjective factors are "in here" in the mind or emotions of the person, whereas objective factors are "out there" in

the physical aspects of the environment. Because time is sequential, either the subject must precede the object or the object must precede the subject. They are forever separated in time.

11. See Slife (1993) for a discussion of alternative assumptions of time.

12. We acknowledge the contribution of Slife (1993) in outlining the themes he found in alternative views of the same temporal characteristics discussed earlier in the chapter.

13. From a holistic perspective, a later event may be part of a complete whole and lends meaning to earlier events; for example, reading to the end of this chapter may cause an overall shift in understanding for the reader from what he would have gleaned reading only the first part of the chapter.

14. Cooperrider & Whitney, 1999a, 1999b.

15. Cooperrider & Whitney, 1999a, 1999b.

16. Slife, 1993.

17. Carl Jung was a Swiss psychiatrist and founder of analytical psychology. See http://en.wikipedia.org/wiki/Synchronicity for a more complete explanation of synchronicity.

18. Piaget in Slife, 1993.

19. Wade, 2006.

20. For example, Laura Berman Fortgang, in her book *Living Your Best Life* (2001), has a wonderful set of questions in her appendixes. In their book *Brief Coaching for Lasting Solutions*, Insoo Kim Berg and Peter Szabo (2005) present powerful questions focused on helping clients find their own solutions.

21. Cooperrider & Whitney, 1999a, 1999b.

22. Slife, 1993.

23. The fusion of linear time with simple cause and effect can be traced back to David Hume in the 1700s, who articulated what has become the classic model for causation based on Newton's concept of time. Causality is seen as occurring in sequence across time, cause having to appear before effect (Lana, 1969). Such explanations of causation based solely on a Newtonian view of time have been

challenged over the years as being too limited. Ludwig von Bertalanffy (1968), the father of systems theory, considered the traditional scientific approach of one-way causality to be insufficient.
He pointed to the appearance in science of such ideas as wholeness,
holism, organicism, and gestalt, all signifying systems of elements in
mutual interaction and not single units lined up like pearls on a
necklace. Quantum mechanics showed a fundamental departure
from classical theory by pointing out how only probabilities can be
predicted, not single events (Prigogine & Stengers, 1984). Complex, self-organizing systems adapt to their environment and live at
the "edge of chaos"—a type of balance point where life has enough
stability to sustain itself and enough creativity to be called life; such
systems are dynamic and spontaneous and cannot be accounted for
in the Newtonian explanation of cause and effect (Waldrop, 1992).

24. Piaget viewed developmental stages in this manner; insight is known
to trigger sudden change; and group or family systems can be altered
by a change in just one person's attitude or behavior (Slife, 1993).

25. Cooperrider & Whitney, 1999a, 1999b.

26. Cooperrider, 1990.

27. Goleman, 1987.

28. Rosenthal & Jacobson, 1968.

29. Goleman, 1987.

30. Bandura, 1994.

31. Chaffee, 2004.

32. Wade, 2006.

Chapter Five

1. Seligman & Csikszentmihalyi, 2000.

2. As inspired by the four-stage approach of Appreciative Inquiry,
which has been well researched and applied in organizations worldwide (see Whitney & Trosten-Bloom, 2003).

3. In AI, careful, thoughtful, and informed attention is given to the
topic of inquiry so that it is positive (or at least neutral), imagina-

tive, and creative. The topic is considered the most important part of any AI project, as the seeds of change are implicit in the very first questions asked (Watkins & Mohr, 2001; Cooperrider & Whitney, 1999a).

4. Brett & Atwater, 2001.

5. Horvath & Symonds, 1991; Horvath & Luborsky, 1993.

6. Brett & Atwater, 2001.

7. Adapted from Walter & Peller, 1992.

8. Lethem, 2002.

9. Berg & Miller, 1992.

Chapter Six

1. Fredrickson, 2003.

2. Isen & Shalker, 1982.

3. Isen & Shalker, 1982.

4. Knowles, Holton, & Swanson, 2005.

5. Clance, 1985.

6. Roberts et al., 2005.

7. An AI reference for those interested in learning more about positive questions is Whitney, Cooperrider, Trosten-Bloom, & Kaplin, 2005.

Chapter Seven

1. There is no universally agreed-on biological or psychological definition of dreaming (see http://en.wikipedia.org/wiki/Dream; Goleman, 1984).

2. Cooperrider, 1990, p. 93.

3. For example, see Gallwey, 1974.

4. Cooperrider, 1990.

5. Richardson, cited in Cooperrider, 1990.

6. Sullivan, cited in Cooperrider, 1990.

7. Cooperrider, 1990.

8. Cousins, cited in Cooperrider, 1990.

9. Rosenthal and Jacobson (1968) conducted a classic study in which teachers were led to have positive images of some students (identified as high potential) and negative images of other students (identified as low potential). In reality, all student groupings were randomly assigned. Over time, subtle changes occurred: the students identified as high potential actually showed increased achievement over the other groups.

10. Cooperrider, 1990.

11. William Shakespeare, *As You Like It*, act 2, scene 7.

12. Judge, 1993.

13. Schön (1979) gave the example of a slum being framed as either a "blight" or as a "community," depending on one's perspective.

14. Barrett & Cooperrider, 2001.

15. Barrett & Cooperrider, 2001, p. 2.

16. Judge, 1993.

17. Srivastva & Barrett, 1988.

18. Watkins & Mohr, 2001.

19. Hastie & Kumar and Darley & Gross, cited in Cooperrider, 1990.

20. Watkins & Mohr, 2001, p. xxxi.

21. Watkins & Mohr, 2001.

22. These questions are adapted from Watkins and Mohr, 2001.

23. Cooperrider, 1990.

24. Rosenthal & Jacobson, 1968.

25. Cooperrider, 1990, p. 98.

26. Wieman, quoted in Cooperrider, 1990, p. 108.

Chapter Eight

1. Whitney & Trosten-Bloom, 2003, p. 198.

2. Jaworski, 1996.

3. Collins & Porras, 1996.

4. Jaworski, 1996.

5. Inspired by Lelas, McClintock, and Zingarella, 2003.

Chapter Nine

1. Cooperrider, Whitney, & Stavros, 2003, p. 177.

2. Williamson, 1992.

3. Cooperrider et al., 2003, p. 181.

4. We acknowledge Cooperrider et al. (2003) for developing the concept of competence, which we have adapted for Appreciative Coaching.

5. Watkins & Mohr, 2001, p. 38.

6. Cooperrider, 1990.

Chapter Ten

1. Koltko-Rivera, 2004.

2. Koltko-Rivera, 2004.

3. Koltko-Rivera (2004) has created a comprehensive model of a worldview; we are focusing on specific aspects of his model rather than presenting it in its entirety.

4. Koltko-Rivera, 2004, p. 20.

5. Koltko-Rivera, 2004.

6. Connerrosberg, 1997.

7. Rokeach, cited in Koltko-Rivera, 2004.

8. Mind mapping was developed by Tony and Barry Buzan, 1994.

9. Keyes & Haidt, 2003.

References

Bandura, A. (1994). Self-efficacy. In V. S. Ramachaudran (Ed.), *Encyclopedia of human behavior* (Vol. 4, pp. 71–81). New York: Academic Press.

Barrett, F., & Cooperrider, D. L. (2001). Generative metaphor intervention: A new approach for working with systems divided by conflict and caught in defensive perception. In D. L. Cooperrider, P. F. Sorensen, T. F. Yaeger, & D. Whitney (Eds.), *Appreciative Inquiry: An emerging direction for organization development* (pp. 121–145). Champaign, IL: Stipes.

Berg, I. K., & Miller, S. D. (1992). *Working with the problem drinker: A solution-focused approach*. New York: Norton.

Berg, I. K., & Szabo, P. (2005). *Brief coaching for lasting solutions*. New York: Norton.

Berger, P. L., & Luckmann, T. (1966). *The social construction of reality*. New York: Doubleday.

Boltz, M. (2006). *The psychology of time*. Retrieved May 24, 2006, from www.haverford.edu/psych/courses/p220/Psy220%20syllabus.htm.

Brett, J. F., & Atwater, L. E. (2001). 360° feedback: Accuracy, reactions, and perceptions of usefulness. *Journal of Applied Psychology, 86*, 930–942.

Buckingham, M., & Coffman, C. (1999). *First, break all the rules: What the world's greatest managers do differently*. New York: Simon & Schuster.

Buzan, T., & Buzan, B. (1994). *The mind map book: How to use radiant thinking to maximize your brain's untapped potential*. New York: Penguin Books.

Caldwell, C. (1996). *Getting our bodies back: Recovery, healing, and transformation through body-centered psychotherapy*. Boston: Shambhala.

Cameron, K. S., Dutton, J. E., & Quinn, R. E. (Eds.). (2003). *Positive Organizational Scholarship: Foundations of a new discipline*. San Francisco: Berrett-Koehler.

Chaffee, P. (2004). *Claiming the light: Appreciative Inquiry and congregational transformation*. Retrieved June 14, 1006, from www.congregationalresources.org/Appreciative/Introduction.asp.

Clance, P. R. (1985). *The impostor phenomenon: Overcoming the fear that haunts your success*. Atlanta: Peachtree.

Clancy, A. L. (1996). *Toward a holistic concept of time: Exploring the link between internal and external temporal experiences*. Unpublished doctoral dissertation, Fielding Graduate University, Santa Barbara, CA.

Collins, J., & Porras, J. (1996, September–October). Building your company's vision. *Harvard Business Review*, pp. 65–77.

Connerrosberg, A. (1997). Humanomics: A qualitative life cycle analysis of adults in midlife who are coping with involuntary job loss: The Connerrosberg self-discovery coping-process. Unpublished doctoral dissertation, Fielding Graduate University, Santa Barbara, CA.

Cooperrider, D. L. (1986). *Appreciative Inquiry: Toward a methodology for understanding and enhancing organizational innovation*. Unpublished doctoral dissertation, Case Western Reserve University, Cleveland, OH.

Cooperrider, D. L. (1990). Positive image, positive action: The affirmative basis of organizing. In S. Srivastva & D. L. Cooperrider (Eds.), *Appreciative management and leadership: The power of positive thought and action in organizations* (pp. 91–125). San Francisco: Jossey-Bass. (A reprint of this chapter can be retrieved from www.stipes.com/aichap2.htm.)

Cooperrider, D. L., & Sekerka, L. E. (2003). Toward a theory of positive organizational change. In K. S. Cameron, J. E. Dutton, & R. E. Quinn (Eds.), *Positive Organizational Scholarship: Foundations in a new discipline* (pp. 225–240). San Francisco: Berrett-Koehler.

Cooperrider, D. L., & Srivastva, S. (1987). Appreciative Inquiry in organizational life. In R. W. Woodman & E. Pasmore (Eds.), *Research in organization change and development: An annual series featuring advances in theory* (Vol. 1, pp. 129–169). Greenwich, CT: JAI Press.

Cooperrider, D. L., & Whitney, D. (1999a). Appreciative Inquiry: A positive revolution in change. In P. Holman & T. Devane (Eds.), *The change handbook: Group methods for shaping the future* (pp. 245–261). San Francisco: Berrett-Koehler.

Cooperrider, D. L., & Whitney, D. (1999b). *Collaborating for change: Appreciative Inquiry*. San Francisco: Berrett-Koehler.

Cooperrider, D. L., & Whitney, D. (2001). A positive revolution in change. In D. L. Cooperrider, P. F. Sorensen, D. Whitney, & T. F. Yaeger (Eds.), *Appreciative Inquiry: An emerging direction for organization development* (pp. 9–29). Champaign, IL: Stipes.

Cooperrider, D. L., Whitney, D., & Stavros, J. M. (2003). *Appreciative Inquiry handbook*. San Francisco: Berrett-Koehler.

Cousins, N. (1983). *The healing heart*. New York: Norton.

Csikszentmihalyi, M. (1990). *Flow: The psychology of optimal experience*. New York: HarperCollins.

Darley, J. M., & Gross, P. H. (1983). A hypothesis-confirming bias in labeling effects. *Journal of Personality and Social Psychology, 44*(1), 20–33.

de Shazer, S., Berg, I. K., Lipchik, E., Nunnally, E., Molnar, A., Gingerich, W., & Weiner-Davis, M. (1986). Brief therapy: Focused solution development. *Family Process, 25*, 207–221.

Diener, E., & Seligman, M.E.P. (2004). Beyond money: Towards an economy of well-being. *Psychological Science in the Public Interest, 5*(1), 1–31.

Doherty, D. R. (1997). The emotional contagion scale: A measure of individual differences. *Journal of Nonverbal Behavior, 21*(2), 131–154.

Dutton, J. E. (2003). *Energize your workplace: How to create and sustain high-quality connections at work*. San Francisco: Jossey-Bass.

Fortgang, L. B. (2001). *Living your best life: Discover your life's blueprint for success*. New York: Penguin Putnam.

Fredrickson, B. L. (1998). What good are positive emotions? *Review of General Psychology, 2*, 300–319.

Fredrickson, B. L. (2003). Positive emotions and upward spirals in organizations. In K. S. Cameron, J. E. Dutton, & R. E. Quinn (Eds.), *Positive Organizational Scholarship: Foundations of a new discipline* (pp. 163–175). San Francisco: Berrett-Koehler.

Gable, S. L., & Haidt, J. (2005). What (and why) is Positive Psychology? *Review of General Psychology, 9*(2), 103–110.

Gallwey, W. T. (1974). *The inner game of tennis*. New York: Bantam Books.

Gertner, J. (2003, September 7). The futile pursuit of happiness. *New York Times Magazine*, p. 45.

Goleman, D. (1984, July 10). Do dreams really contain important secret meaning? *The New York Times*. Retrieved February 27, 2006, from http://select.nytimes.com/gst/abstract.html?resF10813FA385D0C738DDDAE0894DC484D81.

Goleman, D. (1987, February 3). Research affirms power of positive thinking. *The New York Times*. Retrieved February 27, 2006, from http://query.nytimes.com/gst/fullpage.html?sechealth&res9B0DEEDA163EF930A357 51C0A961948260.

Goleman, D. (1995). *Emotional intelligence: Why it can matter more than IQ*. New York: Bantam Books.

Hammond, S. A. (1998). *The thin book of Appreciative Inquiry* (2nd ed.). Plano, TX: Thin Book.

Hastie, R., & Kumar, P. A. (1979). Person memory: Personality traits as organizing principles in memory for behaviors. *Journal of Personality and Social Psychology, 37*(1), 25–38.

Hatfield, E., Cacioppo, J. T., & Rapson, R. L. (1994). *Emotional contagion.* New York: Cambridge University Press.

Horvath, A. O., & Luborsky, L. (1993). The role of the therapeutic alliance in psychotherapy. *Journal of Consulting and Clinical Psychology, 61,* 561–573.

Horvath, A. O., & Symonds, B. D. (1991). Relationship between working alliance and outcome in psychotherapy: A meta-analysis. *Journal of Counseling Psychology, 38*(2), 139–149.

Isen, A. M., & Shalker, T. E. (1982). The effect of feeling state on evaluation of positive, neutral, and negative stimuli: When you "accentuate the positive," do you "eliminate the negative"? *Social Psychology Quarterly, 45*(1), 58–63.

Jaworski, J. (1996). *Synchronicity: The inner path of leadership.* San Francisco: Berrett-Koehler.

Judge, A. (1993). Metaphor as an unexplored catalytic language for global governance. In H. F. Didsbury Jr. (Ed.), *The years ahead: Perils, problems and promises* (pp. 201–207). Bethesda, MD: World Futures Society.

Judge, T. A., & Ilies, R. (2004). Research briefs: Is positiveness in organizations always desirable? *Academy of Management Executive, 18*(4), 151–155.

Keyes, C.L.M., & Haidt, J. (Eds.). (2003). *Flourishing: Positive Psychology and the life well-lived.* Washington, DC: American Psychological Association.

Knowles, M. S., Holton, E. F., & Swanson, R. A. (2005). The adult learner: The definitive classic in adult education and human resource development. Amsterdam: Elsevier.

Koltko-Rivera, M. E. (2004). The psychology of worldviews. *Review of General Psychology, 8*(1), 3–58.

Lana, R. (1969). *Assumptions of social psychology.* New York: Appleton-Century-Crofts.

Lelas, L., McClintock, L., & Zingarella, B. (2003). *Simple steps: 10 weeks to getting control of your life.* New York: New American Library.

Lethem, J. (2002). Brief solution focused therapy. *Child and Adolescent Mental Health, 7*(4), 189–192.

Lewin, K. (1948). *Resolving social conflicts.* New York: HarperCollins.

Luthans, F., & Avolio, B. (2003). Authentic leadership development. In K. S. Cameron, J. E. Dutton, & R. E. Quinn (Eds.), *Positive Organizational Scholarship: Foundations of a new discipline* (pp. 241–258). San Francisco: Berrett-Koehler.

Mohr, B. (2004). *Effecting positive change through Appreciative Inquiry.* Retrieved May 10, 2006, from www.executiveforum.com.

Newton, I. (1990). *Mathematical principles of natural philosophy* (A. Motte, Trans.). (Revised by Florian Cajori). Chicago: University of Chicago Press. (Original work published 1687)

Piaget, J. (1967). *Six psychological studies.* New York: Random House.

Piaget, J. (1970). Piaget's theory. In P. H. Mussen (Ed.), *Manual of child psychology* (3rd ed., Vol. 1, pp. 703–732). Hoboken, NJ: Wiley.

Prigogine, I., & Stengers, I. (1984). *Order out of chaos: Man's new dialogue with nature.* New York: Bantam Books.

Quinn, R. E., & Quinn, G. T. (2002). *Letters to Garrett.* San Francisco: Jossey-Bass.

Rath, T., & Clifton, D. (2004). *How full is your bucket? Positive strategies for work and life.* Princeton, NJ: Gallup Press.

Richardson, A. (1969). *Mental imagery.* New York: Springer.

Rilke, R. M. (1987). *Letters to a young poet.* New York: Vintage Books.

Roberts, L. M., Dutton, J. E., Spreitzer, G. M., Heaphy, E. D., & Quinn, R. E. (2005). Composing the reflected best-self portrait: Building pathways for becoming extraordinary in work organizations. *Academy of Management Review, 30,* 712–736.

Rokeach, M. (1973). *The nature of human values.* New York: Free Press.

Rosenthal, R., & Jacobson, L. (1968). *Pygmalion in the classroom.* Austin, TX: Holt, Rinehart and Winston.

Schön, D. A. (1979). Generative metaphor: A perspective on problem-setting in social policy. In A. Ortony (Ed.), *Metaphor and thought* (pp. 137–163). Cambridge: Cambridge University Press.

Seligman, M.E.P. (2002). *Authentic happiness: Using the new Positive Psychology to realize your potential for lasting fulfillment.* New York: Free Press.

Seligman, M.E.P., & Csikszentmihalyi, M. (2000). Positive Psychology: An introduction. *American Psychologist, 55*(1), 5–14.

Slife, B. (1993). *Time and psychological explanation.* New York: State University of New York Press.

Srivastva, S., & Barrett, F. (1988). The transforming nature of metaphors in group development: A study in group theory. *Human Relations, 41*(1), 31–63.

Sullivan, H. S. (1947). *Conceptions of modern psychiatry.* Washington, DC: William Alanson White Psychiatric Foundation.

von Bertalanffy, L. (1968). *General system theory.* New York: Braziller.

Wade, J. (2006). *Are you asking the right questions?* Retrieved March 16, 2006, from www.stuttering-specialist.com/documents/wade.html.

Waldrop, M. (1992). *Complexity: The emerging science at the edge of order and chaos*. New York: Simon & Schuster.

Walter, J. L., & Peller, J. E. (1992). *Becoming solution focused in brief therapy*. New York: Brunner/Mazel.

Watkins, J. M., & Mohr, B. J. (2001). *Appreciative Inquiry: Change at the speed of imagination*. San Francisco: Jossey-Bass.

Weakland, J. H., Fisch, R., Watzlawick, P., & Bodin, A. M. (1974). Brief therapy: Focused problem resolution. *Family Process, 13*, 141–168.

Wheatley, M. J. (1992). *Leadership and the new science: Learning about organization from an orderly universe*. San Francisco: Berrett-Koehler.

Whitney, D., Cooperrider, D. L., Trosten-Bloom, A., & Kaplin, B. S. (2005). *Encyclopedia of positive questions: Vol. 1. Using Appreciative Inquiry to bring out the best in your organization*. Bedford Heights, OH: Lakeshore Communications.

Whitney, D., & Trosten-Bloom, A. (2003). *The power of Appreciative Inquiry: A practical guide to positive change*. San Francisco: Berrett-Koehler.

Whyte, D. (1994). *The heart aroused: Poetry and the preservation of the soul in corporate America*. New York: Currency/Doubleday.

Wieman, H. N. (1926). *Religious experience and scientific method*. Oxford, England: Macmillan.

Williamson, M. (1992). *A return to love: Reflections on the principles of A Course in Miracles*. New York: HarperCollins.

Wilson, T. D. (2002). *Strangers to ourselves: Discovering the adaptive unconscious*. Cambridge, MA: Belknap Press.

Worline, M. C., & Quinn, R. W. (2003). Courageous principled action. In K. S. Cameron, J. E. Dutton, & R. E. Quinn, (Eds.), *Positive Organizational Scholarship: Foundations of a new discipline* (pp. 138–157). San Francisco: Berrett-Koehler.

Wrzesniewski, A. (2003). Finding positive meaning at work. In K. S. Cameron, J. E. Dutton, & R. E. Quinn (Eds.), *Positive Organizational Scholarship: Foundations of a new discipline* (pp. 296–308). San Francisco: Berrett-Koehler.

Index